12 POWER PRINCIPLES FOR KINGDOM LEADERS

Amanda Goodson

No part of this publication may be reproduced or transmitted in any form or by any means, mechanical or electronic, including photocopying for recording, or by any information storage and retrieval system, without express written permission from the publisher.

ISBN-13: 978-0692422984

ISBN-10: 0692422986

Copyright © 2015 by Dr. Amanda H. Goodson – All Rights Reserved.

Unless otherwise indicated the Scripture quotations are taken from the Spirit Filled Bible, New King James Version. © Copyright 2002, Nelson. Used by permission of Nelson Publishing. All rights reserved.

Printed in the U.S.A.

Second Edition

INTRODUCTION

I was in Washington, D.C., a few years ago at an engineering award conference. At the conference, several people from across the world were honored for their innovations, creativity, and leadership in technology. During one of the sessions, modern technologists were given awards for their contributions and notable achievements in the areas of science, technology, engineering, and mathematics. Also during the session, someone was recognized for his contributions in the area of technological advancements in Africa and the United States.

I noticed that there was something special about this particular gentleman. He carried himself differently. His personal presence illuminated the whole room, as if he was a bright light sent for others to see. He was dressed professionally, like a business president or CEO, in a suit that was perfectly tailored for him. His executive staff stood erect when he entered and opened up a path for him to walk to the stage. As he walked onto the stage, I noticed the excellence with which he handled receiving his special honor. When he said his acceptance speech, his voice exuded great influence and authority. His tone and pitch were deep like many rivers of water and reverberated like a symphony of waves rushing in cadence in an ocean. He stood like a person who deserved honor—with his shoulders erect and with perfect posture and poise like a presidential candidate or elected official. When he was presented to the audience, he was announced as a king of an African country. I will call him King "A."

At the time of this event, I was studying about the Kingdom that God owns, which includes everything—even the territory over which King A resided and was overseer. I came to know that King A knew about God's Kingdom and acted accordingly. His actions were just reflecting exactly what the Word of God says. God owns it all and sent His wonderful Son Jesus to get it all back for us to multiply and to enjoy, rule, bear fruit, and subdue.

We are all meant to walk through our lives as confidently as King A, and you can do so through your relationship with Christ Jesus. In this book, you will discover God's Kingdom through Scripture, and the Holy Spirit in you will guide you to all truth. In God's Kingdom, your way of thinking and attitude must match what His Word declares about you in order to be effective in His Kingdom. The Holy Spirit in you will transform and infuse you with much power because, as a son or daughter, you have unlimited access to God, as you govern His territory.

If you want to reinvigorate your experience or be exposed to the sovereign reign and rule of a king over his territory, including his governing influence over that domain, this book will enlighten, encourage, and comfort you as you walk boldly declaring His divine Kingship and Lordship through Christ Jesus.

This book will allow you to experience God's nature and desire toward all of His people and to affect every believer. In fact, the purpose for each believer is to know God and His Kingdom.

Enjoy this book, and let the Holy Spirit enliven you again and bring hope through faith in your life. You will accomplish great things for the Kingdom–so go forth!

CONTENTS

Introduction

1. Kingdom Genomes — 7
2. Kingdom Citizenship and Kingship — 13
3. Kingdom Mindset: Thinking Like a King — 21
4. Kingdom Attitude — 29
5. Kingdom Character — 39
6. Transforming You—Power Reinstated — 61
7. Kingdom Atmosphere — 69
8. Keys to the Kingdom—Unlimited Access — 75
9. Governing Influence — 79
10. The Kingdom-Lordship Principle — 87
11. Stewardship—Not Ownership — 93
12. Assuming Your Position of Kingdom Leadership — 101

Conclusion — 109

End Notes — 113

About the Author — 116

Chapter 1
Kingdom Genomes

"So God created man in His own image, in the image of God He created him; male and female He created them." (Genesis 1:27)

Foundational to any concept of Kingdom Leadership is the reality that God created you in His own image. We were created by God's divine design, and with His unconditional love and grace we were each made physically diverse in order to complete God's authorized decree to multiply and have dominion over the earth. **All** that you are was designed for Kingdom purpose. Some people question why they are a certain body type, why they have a certain skin color, or why their hair is curly or straight. Instead of doubting your value because of a supposed flaw, look again to see that your physical characteristics are just evidence of the Kingdom genome. Instead of doubting, ask how God intends to use His reflection in you to accomplish Kingdom business.

Humans were the only part of creation imparted with God's likeness and image. "God is not confined to human form; but imperfect and finite man shares in His nature," in particular His attributes of life, personality, truth, wisdom, love, holiness, and justice.[1] With God reserving these attributes for humans, know that something more than special is the very basis for your creation.

Genome is a scientific term that describes a complete set of genetic material that makes an organism. It is the complete code that shows what we are made of. Essentially, our Kingdom genome is what God put into us. The physical genome can identify structural similarities that identify how we genetically develop as people.[2] Packed within our Kingdom genome is the code that lays out how we are to evolve as Kingdom leaders doing Kingdom work.

Kingdom genomes are what qualify, justify, and solidify your inherited position of authority in the earth realm. If we think in terms of what happens with a baby in the womb, we can see just how miraculous the Kingdom genome is.

As soon as a life is formed in the womb, the cells of the new life begin to multiply and then specialize into what they are to become—a brain, a heart, bones, muscles, etc. Life expands, but within controlled limits. Only so many cells will be made. Only certain types of cells will be made. It is the genome, the DNA, that drives this process. Likewise, in God's Kingdom, we are specialized to be just what He wants us to be; nothing more and nothing less.

Scientists have decoded the human genome. They have looked at the code to determine the sequences that are responsible for making us who we are. The human genome can even be used to tell us much about our ancestors, the people who made us in the earthly realm.

The Kingdom genome shows that we were made in God's image. The *Complete Word Study Old Testament* gives the definition of God's image (6754 Tselem) as the following: "God made man in such a way as to reflect some of His own perfections–perfect in knowledge, righteousness, and holiness, with dominion over the creatures. ...it is only the shadow of a thing, representing the original in an imprecise manner, lacking the essential characteristics (reality) of the original. ...Even though man has been tarnished by sin as a result of the Fall, he still maintains the essential nature of God."[3]

The human reality is that we were created in the image of God, and although we are commanded to be holy as God is holy, humans are fallible. I believe this is the reason why the Word instructs us to seek the Lord daily through prayer and study of the Word, and to place God first in all things and not conform to the world. Because we are fallible, we have the ability to change our thinking and our behavior, depending upon who or what things are within our circle of influence. It is possible that the choices we make can have the effect of changing and impacting future generations.

A genomic change in the physical body can be the result of something inherited from our ancestors. These changes, or inherited alterations, are called mutations and may happen between generations or may occur over a lifetime. We inherit mutations from our parents, but mutations are happening within our cellular structure all the time. Environmental factors, such as cigarette smoking and sunlight, can increase the rate of DNA mutations.

Our spiritual environment can have elements that can be just as altering as the environmental factors affecting physical DNA. Scientists say that some mutations might be minimized with the proper diet or by living in environments that aren't polluted. Exercise is also important in protecting the genome against mutations. A healthy person has a certain look, even a glow. The same can be said about the Kingdom genome.

Kingdom genomes represent the spiritually inherited DNA structure that we have received from God. We, too, can be subject to spiritual mutations. When we expose ourselves to the environmental factor of sin, we can begin to show signs of spiritual illness. It is the threat of sin, of mutations to our Kingdom genome, that necessitates a strong prayer life and one being steeped in the Word of God. We can understand these practices as exercise to maintain a strong Kingdom genome. We have to take care of God's image. When we are doing the work to take care of our Kingdom genomes, others can tell because we are reflecting God. It is in our Kingdom genome that we are to be of God's image. To keep it that way, we have to pray, read God's Word, and worship.

In later chapters, we will discuss how it is that we are Kingdom citizens and actual kings. However, it is the Kingdom genome that is the beginning of it all. Citizenship is a matter taken up at birth, but the genome is at play at the first spark of life. As a starting point, it is important for you to know that God designed you to look like Him. His mechanism for doing this was his Kingdom genome. In addition, God was concerned about where you would be.

It is God's will that produces salvation, not our human will. Those who receive Jesus as Savior and His Word are guaranteed full authority to claim the exalted title of being God's children. We receive His Name, and as the recipient of His Name, we are automatically heirs of His character. We were created to reflect His perfection in the earth realm. That perfection is, therefore, represented in our position of righteousness and holiness as we are seated with God in heavenly places and are able to exercise our authority and dominion over His creation.

Chapter 2
Kingdom Citizenship and Kingship

When I was born, I had no choice in what would be my country of citizenship. My parents were residents and citizens of the United States and decided to remain so. (I am glad that they did.) Thus, I became a citizen of my country merely by the choice of my parents.

A different kind of citizenship is a focus of this book, and it is of a type that requires personal choice. It doesn't require that you relinquish citizenship in your country of origin. You can retain your earthly citizenship, but in Kingdom citizenship, you have the opportunity to experience rights and privileges that earthly nations cannot provide.

To help with our understanding of Kingdom citizenship, think about the example of my earthly citizenship. How did I become a citizen of the United States—through my parents. The Scripture clearly teaches that we are members of God's family and just how it is that we became so. First, God sent his son through channels that we easily recognize. He was born of a mother just like we were. He was even born within the law of Jewish custom.

> *"God sent forth His Son, born of a woman, born under the law, to redeem those who were under the law."*

Now, here is the part that tells us just why God sent His son:

> *"To redeem those who were under the law that we might receive the adoption as sons."*

There is more:

> *"And because you are sons, God has sent forth the Spirit of His Son into your hearts, crying out, 'Abba Father!' Therefore you are no longer a slave but a son, and if a son, then <u>an heir of God through Christ</u>."*
> *(Galatians 4:4-7)*

So the message is clear—if you are a believer in Jesus Christ, you are "an heir of God through Christ." We are heirs to God's Kingdom. We are Kingdom citizens.

Many people misunderstand Jesus Christ and the people who operate as Kingdom citizens. Misunderstanding Jesus Christ, His timing, and His purpose for coming has caused many conflicts among many religions and secular groups. This misunderstanding keeps many away from the benefits of being a Kingdom citizen, but it is likely that the greatest misunderstanding comes from those who claim to be His representatives. Far too often, His representatives misrepresent Him and how it is that they are Kingdom citizens.

This is unfortunate because people who truly operate in their full Kingdom citizenship, as heirs to God's Kingdom, have the power and authority to be the most influential people. In this book, I outline 12 principles that Kingdom leaders live out. However, before we dive into the rest of these powerful principles, let's establish some basics about the Kingdom.

Kingdom Domain

A kingdom is basically a place where a king rules. In the case of God's Kingdom, God is both King and Creator.

> *"... the LORD God made the earth and the heavens, before any plant of the field was in the earth and before any herb of the field had grown." (Genesis 2:4b)*

By virtue of God being the Creator of all things, He is automatically the owner of all things. That makes Him the King over all in the universe (seen and unseen). We are also reminded of God's Kingdom in Psalms:

> *"The earth is the LORD's, and all its fullness, the world and those who dwell therein." (Psalm 24:1)*

He is Lord over all territories and *domains* and is the Sovereign Ruler.

Domain = the land that a ruler or a government controls.[1]

He is the King over His domain; hence we get the term *kingdom*.

Kingdom =

1. the spiritual reign or authority of God (God Himself); and

2. a country, state or territory ruled by a king or queen (those who represent God).

Kingdom synonyms include realm, domain, country, empire, principality, land, nation, state, province, and territory. Other terms are also important in our discussion of the kingdom concept. *Dominion* is one of them.

Kingdom Dominion

We have already established Kingdom citizenship as a component of the Kingdom. This citizenship came with responsibilities. The overarching concept that encapsulates all responsibilities is dominion.

"Then God said, 'Let Us make man in Our image, according to Our likeness; let them have <u>dominion</u> over the fish of the sea, over the birds of the air, and over the cattle, over all the earth and over every creeping thing that creeps on the earth.'" (Genesis 1:26)

Dominion = Sovereignty; control or exercise of control.[2]

We are to have dominion over God's Kingdom. Jesus Christ reiterates in the Gospel of Luke that God has given us the Kingdom:

"Do not fear, little flock, for it is your Father's good pleasure to give you the kingdom." (Luke 12:32)

Thus, yes, we are Kingdom citizens, but we are even more than citizens; we are kings. Our kingship is legal and legitimate. God made it so in giving us the earth. He made Adam a king, and He made Eve a queen equal to Adam in every way. The dominion of the earth is mankind's legal right, power, and authority of rulership. When God said, "Let them have dominion," He transferred the legal rights of the earth to us.[3]

By definition, kingship represents the position, power, province, or prerogative of a king. A king is the central element to a kingdom, and he is the only source of authority within his kingdom. Man's kingship is by divine privilege. God's Kingship is different. He controls the domain because He was the One Who created it. He rules it by creative rights. We rule it because of privilege; it was God's pleasure to give it to us. God gave us rulership but not absolute ownership. Any ownership that we have is the sovereignty that God gave us within our earthly dominion.[3]

The concept above is relative to the Scripture:

> **"The highest heavens belong to the LORD, but the earth he has given to man." (Psalm 115:16, NIV)**

Also, in the garden, God asked for us to take care of His creation. We are to rule it, subdue it, be fruitful, and multiply everything in it.

When God said that He would give dominion to man, he gave the very first command and mandate given to man by his Creator, which was that he would establish a government, or a kingdom, on the earth in order to destroy the chaos and to maintain order. God is the Creator and King; man, in cooperation with Him, became king as His earthly governing representative.

The Word of God clearly states that our God, who is God, is the King and Sovereign Ruler over all things, and He has given His elect the dominion and authority as His representative kings in the earth realm.

> *"May you be blessed by the LORD, Who made heaven and earth. The heaven, even the heavens, are the LORD's; but <u>the earth He has given to the children of men</u>." (Psalm 115:15-16)*

I think you get the picture that we are meant to rule the world, literally. From the very beginning, the purpose of man was to exercise dominion over this Kingdom, the earth. This dominion was to be man's desire. Without dominion, man would have no passion for his efforts. In God's plan, dominion was to be the basis for man's contentment, for his peace. In addition, dominion offered man the fundamental tool needed to fulfill his Kingdom mandate by validating his need for power.

The Fall of mankind was the result of man rebelliously declaring his independence from God and from His heavenly government. The immediate result of this rebellion was social and spiritual chaos, as well as anarchy. From that day to the present, man has been futilely and ineffectively attempting to establish a type of self-government to try to deliver himself out of the chaos that he was actually responsible for creating himself.

Before man could be fully restored to the Kingdom that he had relinquished, his rebellion and sin against God had to be settled and dealt with. Jesus Christ deals with this sin by sacrificing Himself, and in the process showing Himself to be King. In the Old Testament, the prophet Isaiah tells us that our Savior, Jesus Christ will be over the Kingdom:

"For unto us a Child is born, unto us a Son is given; and the <u>government</u> will be upon His shoulder. And His Name will be called Wonderful, Counselor, Mighty God, Everlasting Father, Prince of Peace. Of the increase of <u>His government</u> and peace there will be no end, upon the throne of David and over <u>His Kingdom</u>, to order it and establish it with judgment and justice from that time forward, even forever. The zeal of the Lord of hosts will perform this." (Isaiah 9:6-7)

The death of God's Son Jesus on the cross was the settlement for man's sin; restoring us and putting us back in right standing with God. It was the cross that transferred us back into the Kingdom and restored us to our right positions as sons and daughters of the King.

We now see how we are kings by spiritual lineage. Even after we renounced our kingship in the Fall, it was restored in the sacrificing act of Jesus Christ. However, being fully restored to the Kingdom of God requires that we be able to, not only resume our rightful position, but be able to speak, think, and behave like a king as well. In the next chapter, I reveal how we can develop a Kingdom mindset to do just that.

Thoughts for Kingdom Citizenship and Kingship:

In the space below, list some personal thoughts about how you can exercise your rights as a Kingdom citizen and as a king.

Chapter 3
Kingdom Mindset: Thinking Like a King

Since childhood, we have seen images of royalty in the finest robes and in lavish palaces. Their lives are handled with the strictest protocol. Appearance is highly valued. In Old Testament law, protocol was of the highest importance as well, but the overwhelming message of Jesus Christ is to act from the heart. Even so, Jesus did not drop the essence of the Kingdom mindset. However, when we think in a way consistent with the Kingdom of God, we maintain a mindset that is unlike what you will find in any earthly kingdom.

Thinking, speaking, and behaving like a king in God's Kingdom may not look like or resemble the thoughts, words and behavior of kings that we may be accustomed to seeing. When we begin to have a Kingdom mindset, we will begin to be conscious of the fact that God is our Lord and Savior, and He is also Ruler and has a plan for our lives. He wants to be the One who impacts and influences our lives.[2]

The first step to developing a Kingdom mindset is to be exposed to Kingdom thinking. Jesus Christ acknowledges this as a crucial step in a conversation with his disciples:

"And the disciples came and said to Him, 'Why do You speak to them in parables?' He answered and said to them, 'Because it has been given to you to know the mysteries of the kingdom of heaven, but to them it has not been given. For whoever has, to him more will be given, and he will have abundance; but whoever does not have, even what he has will be taken away from him. Therefore I speak to them in parables, because seeing they do not see, and hearing they do not hear, nor do they understand.'" (Matthew 13: 10-13)

God has graciously given His representatives the ability to comprehend spiritual truths. Those who do not represent Him are faced with the natural consequence of their own rebellion and unbelief, and their own lack of true relationship with God–spiritual blindness (v. 13).

Once people are exposed to the Kingdom mindset and they grab onto it and continue to develop, they tend to share a set of characteristics that I will share with you in this chapter.

Those with a Kingdom mindset continue in faith.

The prerequisite for man being able to fully operate as God's kings in this earth realm is that we continue in faith.

"And you, who once were alienated and enemies in your mind by wicked works, yet now He has reconciled in the body of His flesh through death, to present you holy, and blameless, and above reproach in His sight—

> *if indeed you continue in the faith, grounded and steadfast, and are not moved away from the hope of the gospel which you heard, which was preached to every creature under heaven, of which I, Paul, because a minister."* **(Colossians 1:21-23)**

When this occurs and when we are in complete accord with Him, everything has its proper place. All those who have been reconciled to God have the ability to persevere in faith and obedience because they have been declared righteous and made new creatures (see 2 Cor. 5:17). They have a new disposition that now loves God, hates sin, and desires obedience. They are infused with the indwelling of the Holy Spirit. Their proper place in Him, which is the foundation resting on Christ, allows them to remain solid and faithful by God's enabling grace.

Those with a Kingdom mindset know the message.

To think like the kings we were created to be, we must know Jesus's predominant message. His primary focus was in restoring mankind back into the Kingdom so that we could have all rights and privileges as Kingdom citizens and be able to operate with full authority and purpose.

Your success in the Kingdom of God requires knowing the Word of God. In order to represent Him, you must know the types of things that He would say, the types of things He would do, and you must know and understand the magnitude of His power and authority and be able to act on His behalf; just as He would act. We have the ability to act on His behalf without any fear or intimidation. We have been given the authority of God to have power over ALL of Satan's power. Not only that, but we have His promise that nothing shall injure us.

The weapon that God has given us to combat any lie or attack of the enemy is His Word. This is why it is so important that the people of God pray, study, and meditate on the Word. The Scriptures refer to the Word as the "sword of the Spirit" (see Ephesians 6:17), and Jesus says that the Word is "spirit and life" (see John 6:63), which means that His Word represents an actual reality–it is the living Spirit of the Kingdom of God.

Know that, according to God's Word, your kingship is permanent; it's forever. A king is always a king by virtue of birthright; he or she is born into the position and has inherent authority. There are no 'elected' kings. Elections are conducted within republic and democratic forms of government such as in the United States, where the majority of the electorate elects a candidate. The majority rules in these elections. Because there are no elections, a king cannot be voted out of his office. A king rules for life. The power and authority that you exercise on behalf of the Lord has no expiration. This thought in itself should give you boldness to move forward in executing God's plan for your life.

Those with a Kingdom mindset seek the Kingdom.

In the following Scripture, Jesus compels us to seek the Kingdom first.

> ***"But seek first the kingdom of God and His righteousness…" (Matthew 6:33a)***

This command infers that we may have sought after other things besides the Kingdom, and now we are to establish ourselves in the proper order and take our rightful positions.

In order to represent the King, we are required to know His plan and be able to articulate and communicate it.

Those with a Kingdom mindset seek righteousness.

Jesus said to seek the righteousness of the Kingdom (Matthew 6:33a). Seeking God's righteousness is seeking after His moral character and desiring to conform to all He commands and appoints. His righteousness is imputed and imparted as a gift to man. It is not something that man could have earned or established on his own. We are filled with what we seek after. Our hunger and thirst can be satisfied with a right relationship with Him.

> *"Blessed are those who hunger and thirst for righteousness." (Matthew 5:6)*

Those with a Kingdom mindset have a Kingdom response.

To have a Kingdom mindset is to have a fixed mental attitude or a disposition, being able to respond to the situations that you may face. We are products of what we think most (see Proverbs 23:7). This is the reason prayer is so critical and why God needs us to pray. The only time He will be released to intervene in earth matters is when we pray and ask Him to do so. He has given His people sovereignty over the earth; but when we call upon His Name, all of heaven will invade our territory on our behalf.

> *"And I will give you the keys of the kingdom of heaven, and whatever you bind on earth will be bound in heaven, and whatever you loose on earth will be loosed in heaven." (Matthew 16:19)*

A true king is confident in his or her rulership (Yes, some kings are actually women). A true king will not ever allow anything or anyone to usurp or seize any parts of his or her domain. Subversive and rebellious attacks are not tolerated, as shown in the Scripture below:

> *"For though we walk in the flesh, we do not war according to the flesh. For the weapons of our warfare are not carnal but mighty in God for pulling down strongholds, casting down arguments and every high thing that exalts itself against the knowledge of God, bringing every thought into captivity to the obedience of Christ." (2 Corinthians 10:3-5)*

Your Kingdom authority, granted by God, has provided you with all of the spiritual resources required for every threat or trial. And because the God we serve is without limits and is the Maker of heaven and earth, this means that you have an unlimited supply of everything that you need in the Kingdom.

Those who have a Kingdom mindset know their sphere of influence.

This Kingship authority is not to be taken lightly. We are responsible for the management of God's Kingdom. That means that all things, whether they be good or evil, are our responsibility, and our rulership is reflected in the nature and quality of our management.

As His representatives, it is important to keep in mind that God gives each of us his or her own kingdom or sphere of influence. Your sphere happens to be wherever God wants to establish His purpose.

The governing impact of God's will over a particular territory is His Kingdom. He has chosen to influence the earth through His chosen people. Therefore, as His representatives, we have the responsibility of influencing others everywhere we go and in everything we do. The territory that you rule is important to God. He created it, and now you have rulership over it, for Him.

A king owns territory and has a domain. If a king has no territory over which to rule, he cannot be called a king, and therefore, cannot have dominion. The riches of a kingdom measure the affluence of the king, and the king's affluence is measured by the status of the citizens within his realm.

Examine your sphere of influence, your Kingdom. What is the status of its wealth? This is not just a financial question, although finances may be a factor. Overall, what is the spiritual health of those around you? God has positioned you in this domain. Are there strongholds in your Kingdom? On the subject of strongholds, the Word of God shows us how the Kingdom mindset is different from the mindset of an earthly king.

Historically, a king's prowess was marked by wealth and success in war. The king's power came down to who had the best armor, the best technology in weaponry, and the fiercest fighters. As noted previously, as kings of God's Kingdom, our weapons are for:

"...pulling down strongholds, casting down arguments and every high thing that exalts itself against the knowledge of God, bringing every thought into captivity to the obedience of Christ." (2 Corinthians 10:3-5)

Developing a Kingdom mindset takes deliberate effort. Inheriting the Kingdom of God is just the first step in becoming a Kingdom leader. Imagine a young man who has lived a life of poverty, and he is told that he is actually the son of the king. It is now his time to rule. Do you think that the young man will have the mindset of a king? A Kingdom mindset needs to be developed. Practicing the concepts in this chapter will help you to operate in the fullness of your kingship.

Thoughts for Kingdom Mindset/Kingdom Thinking:

In the space below, list some personal reflections about the type of Kingdom thinking you would like to cultivate and develop and how you will begin thinking like a king.

Chapter 4
Kingdom Attitude

In the Kingdom, the right attitude is imperative. So far, we have discussed what it means to have Kingdom DNA or the Kingdom genome, what it means to be a Kingdom citizen and king, and what it is to have a Kingdom mindset. In general, citizenship is about knowing what you have a right to do in the space that you inhabit. Earthly kings know that they have more rights and privileges than the regular citizen. Whether citizens of a particular country or the king, people develop thoughts about how they are to conduct themselves on the basis of their station in life. Essentially, they develop a certain mindset about who they are, what they are capable of doing, and what is within their right to do.

Kingdom citizens, who happen to also be kings, also have a certain mindset about who they are, what they are capable of doing, and what is within their right to do. Emanating from this mindset is a certain attitude in how they conduct themselves in the world. They conduct themselves in a way very consistent with the Kingdom mindset.

Previously, we mentioned that some people misunderstand Kingdom citizenship. Attitude is one area of considerable misunderstanding. Some people construe a Kingdom attitude as arrogant. However, a Kingdom attitude is far different from that of arrogance or pride. In fact, a Kingdom attitude is confidence meshed with humility, while exhibiting noble dignity.

The Apostle Paul gets at this attitude when he says:

"For the Kingdom of God is not eating and drinking, but <u>righteousness</u> and <u>peace</u> and <u>joy</u> in the Holy Spirit. For he who serves Christ in these things is acceptable to God and approved by men." (Romans 14:17-18)

You might have heard the saying, "Attitude is everything." Of course, there are those who proclaim that they are Kingdom leaders, but their actions are consumed with belittling others. That is not the Kingdom way. Kingdom attitude is not having a concern for the external observances, ceremonies, or fulfillments [eating and drinking].

When we think of the concept of a Kingdom, we think of the highest level of living. In order to live in God's highest, we have to incorporate several attributes into our daily practice. We don't have to guess at what these attributes are. Paul is kind enough to state clearly what we can do to live a Kingdom life.

Paul tells us that we can build a Kingdom attitude with righteous living. We had some hint of this in Chapter 3 with Jesus's admonition to seek the Kingdom of God and His righteousness. They go together. Early kingdoms have been noted for their wealth as evidenced by lavish feasts and grand palaces. But in God's Kingdom, righteousness is key.

Righteousness

Righteousness is a word that appears repeatedly throughout the Bible and is frequently mentioned in Christian circles, but few ever stop to say just what righteousness is. Simply put, righteousness is living in a holy and obedient way. If we have our sights on developing a Kingdom attitude, we have in the forefront of our minds this concept of righteousness or holy and obedient living.

Because we believe God, we are accounted by him as righteous.

Peace

Another essential component to developing a Kingdom attitude is to have peace. People who have constant drama in their lives are not living the Kingdom life. If they always have to have the last word in a dispute, they are not operating in a Kingdom attitude. To have an attitude of peace is to have loving tranquility that is produced by the Holy Spirit. Our level of peace characterizes our relationship with God and others. Who would pass up the benefits of a Kingdom by engaging in hostile and volatile relationships? The more peaceful one's attitude, the more the person is surrounded by peace. This is how kingdom living works. Paul indicates a little of this phenomenon in saying that serving Christ in this way ultimately means that God is pleased and other people are pleased. That sounds like peace.

Joy

An attitude of joy also yields benefits in Kingdom living. Joy should not be confused with happiness. Happiness is fleeting. A difficult situation might defeat and deflate someone who is depending on happiness. However, joy is steadfast. Joy in the Holy Spirit is equal to confidence with an attitude of praise and thanksgiving, regardless of physical circumstances.

A good place to find more guidance on the Kingdom attitude is the Beatitudes.[1]

> *"Blessed is the poor in spirit for theirs is the Kingdom of heaven. Blessed are those who mourn, for they shall be comforted. Blessed are the meek, for they shall inherit the earth. Blessed are those who hunger and thirst for righteousness, for they shall be filled. Blessed are the merciful, for they shall obtain mercy. Blessed are the pure in heart, for they shall see God. Blessed are the peacemakers, for they shall be called the sons of God. Blessed are those who are persecuted for righteousness' sake, for theirs is the kingdom of heaven." (Matthew 5:3-10)*

The Beatitudes show just how Kingdom living according to God is different from Kingdom living according to man. To be "poor in spirit" sounds pretty depressing at first, but a true understanding of these words will show what is meant here. To be poor in spirit is to have deep humility. Those who show deep humility toward God are acknowledging that they are not self-sufficient. The Beatitudes tell us that those who are poor in spirit will have the Kingdom of heaven. The meaning of some of the other terms used in the Beatitudes might not be readily apparent. These attributes are necessary for a Kingdom attitude, but they require some explaining, which I have done for you below.

The Right Attitude with the Beatitudes

- <u>Poor in spirit:</u>
  One who is poor in spirit exhibits deep humility and recognizes how utterly spiritual bankrupt he or she is apart from God. To be poor in spirit is the direct opposite of self-sufficiency. One seeking to be poor in spirit is acutely aware of his or her own lostness and hopelessness apart from God's divine grace.

- <u>Mourning:</u>
  Those who mourn are ones mourning over sin and possessing the godly sorrow necessary to produce repentance. They seek correction, and the comfort they receive is that of forgiveness and salvation.

- <u>Meek:</u>
  Meekness is power under control, and it is the opposite of being out of control. Meekness is not synonymous to weakness, but rather it is supreme self-control that is empowered by the Spirit. One who seeks to be meek has an attitude or spirit that accepts God's dealings with them as being good and does not resist or dispute.

- <u>Hunger and thirst for righteousness:</u>
  One thirsting and hungering for righteousness is desiring to be in a right relationship with God and desiring His righteousness, rather than trying to establish his or her own. They are in passionate pursuit of God, which is the opposite of the self-righteousness that was demonstrated by the Pharisees. They know that what they seek will fill them, and they are fully satisfied in receiving that right relationship.

- Merciful:
  One who seeks to be merciful is one who has the ability to be loving, compassionate, and forgiving and demonstrates the ability to show pity for the sufferings of other, just as Christ demonstrated for us when He gave His life as a sacrifice for our sins. The true demonstration of one who seeks to be merciful can be seen in the individual who has the ability to present himself herself as a living sacrifice, as stated in Romans 12:1.

  "Therefore, I urge you, brothers and sisters, in view of God's mercy, to offer your bodies as a living sacrifice, holy and pleasing to God—this is your true and proper worship." (NIV)

- Pure in heart:
  Those seeking to be pure in heart are ones desiring to be God's personal possession and not ones who are self-seeking. They are free of all selfish intentions, and their desire to see God is not only with their perception of faith, but also in the glory of heaven.

- Peacemaker:
  The individual seeking to be a peacemaker is one who is living a peaceful life and has the ability to bring peace to others. Not only is there a desire to make peace between two parties, but there is also a willingness to spread the good news of the peace of God that has been personally experienced.

- Persecuted for the sake of righteousness:
  The willingness to be a follower of Christ comes with the knowledge of being persecuted for His sake.

Persecution, per se, is generally not something to be sought, but when evil is spoken falsely against a follower of Christ, that persecution carries with it the blessing of God.

This is a book about leadership. Some people have a false impression of good leadership. Some people think that effective leaders are those who are feared, so much so that those around them always have the best news to share, even if that news isn't the truth. For some, a real leader is wealthy and has all the best things in life. The Bible warns against these kinds of attitudes.

"Woe to you who are rich, for you have received your consolation. Woe to you who are full, for you shall hunger. Woe to you who laugh now, for you shall mourn and weep. Woe to you when all men speak well of you, for so did their fathers to the false prophets."
(Luke 6:24-26)

By itself, financial wealth is not a sin. Unfortunately, some people are so focused on their wealth and their things that they don't have room for people. Also, a good leader welcomes feedback, even when it doesn't shine the best light on the situation. The Scripture warns that those who are consumed with the stereotypical markers of leadership will eventually have a rude awakening.

The importance of the Kingdom attitude requires knowing how a Kingdom citizen should carry himself or herself. Whereas the attributes in the beatitudes aren't usually associated with leadership but should be, pride and arrogance are often associated with leadership, and shouldn't be. They have no place in the Kingdom.

Pride can be understood in at least two ways. Psychologists have defined two types as *authentic pride* and *hubristic pride*.[2]

- Authentic pride arises when we feel good about ourselves—confident and productive. This type of pride is related to socially desirable personality traits such as being agreeable, conscientious, and emotionally stable.
- Hubristic pride tends to involve egotism and arrogance, and has undesirable traits such as being disagreeable, aggressive, having low or brittle self-esteem, and being prone to shame.

Psychologists believe that people who are trying to improve their self-esteem are essentially trying to generate feelings of authentic pride rather than hubristic pride. They do believe that both of these types of pride, however, can afford someone status in other people's eyes. The status that a Kingdom citizen should be seeking to attain is one of being righteous in the eyes of the Lord; being the king that God created you to be.

What type of character do you seek to have, and in whose eyes does your status find its importance? Is it that of your peers or friends, your employer, or your co-workers? Is it perhaps someone in your family or in the community, or perhaps it's a goal or a lifelong ambition that you seek? If any of these carry more weight or are of greater importance to you than what the Lord would have for you, then seeking the Kingdom first may not have been your first priority.

Thoughts for Kingdom Attitude:

In the space below, list some additional reflections you have about the type of Kingdom attitude you would like to have and about being open to seeking God's Kingdom and His righteousness first.

Chapter 5
Kingdom Character

For the Kingdom minded, character is having God-focused thoughts or qualities. These thoughts or qualities are generated in your inner being and nurtured by your environment and circumstances. The character of God can be expressed outwardly only when it has first been formed in you.

To become like God in character may seem like an unachievable goal, but He always gives us the ability to do all that He has called us to do. The goal must be that we choose to conform to the character of Jesus Christ and Him alone. Any outside influence or teaching that does not fully support this goal and singular purpose cannot be permitted to have rulership over us.

As Kingdom citizens, we are to work on those things that bring value to the Kingdom. From these efforts, we will be able to produce some awesome things for God's Kingdom. When we have Kingdom character, we ourselves expand, as does the environment around us. I believe wholeheartedly that God has called us to grow and to be dynamic people.

An individual possessing Kingdom character has to also have the following traits and abilities:

- **K**eeps Kingdom agenda
- **I**nspires others
- **N**ever gives up
- **G**ives
- **D**ominates territory and destiny
- **O**pens his or her mind to learn
- **M**aintains merchant mentality
- **C**ommits
- **H**umbles himself or herself
- **A**ligns thoughts with high altitude
- **R**epents
- **A**ligns strategically with purpose
- **C**ultivates his or her full range
- **T**akes action
- **E**ndures
- **R**isks for the Kingdom

In the following sections, I show how these traits are borne out in Scripture.

Keeps Kingdom Agenda

As I mentioned in one of my other books, "It is interesting to me that we are called to have a kingly agenda, yet we are not fully aware of how to do it."[1] An agenda is simply a list of tasks that must be completed. As a kingdom citizen, you have a list that is just for you to complete. The great news about this is that you don't have to be fully aware of how you will complete the list today. We have the Holy Spirit to guide us and show us the way. "The Holy Spirit will serve as our Teacher, our Revealer, our Counselor, and He will give us wisdom, understanding and might to do the task."[2]

You will be shaped into the person who can accomplish your assigned kingdom agenda, which will serve God's overall agenda. The Book of Romans tells us that if we focus on God, He will change us from the inside out. This metamorphosis occurs so that we might do the work that He needs us to do, His Kingdom agenda. Perhaps, an illustration can help you to understand how God changes us from the inside.

On one Sunday, I took some beach balls to church. Everyone in the church, both young and mature, had one. I asked everyone to look at the beach ball in their hands. I said, "As you look at the beach ball, you will notice that it is multicolored and multifaceted. It has its own style and own look. Without air, it's flat and a piece of nothing, but the air that you breathe into it gives it its character. The air molds it and shapes it. The ball takes the shape that the owner and manufacturer have already determined." Filled up to its planned shape, the ball can now fulfill its purpose. It can bounce around or soar through the air, as it was designed to do.

What is your bounce? What has God designed you to do? He gives us everything we need for life, eternity, and harmony as he breathes into us. He wants for us to embrace what he is doing in our lives. He breathes into us so that we can take the shape that He designed for us in the beginning so that we can execute the work of His Kingdom.

I don't know what God has planned for you specifically, but I do know that God is calling us to love deeply and to practice loving from a place of leadership or support. Your special agenda will require that you extend God's love to others. Hold onto the Kingdom character of love. If you hold fast to God's love within you, you won't burn out from the challenges of leadership although you will work very hard.

Inspires Others

Someone who has Kingdom character definitely has the ability to inspire others. A good example is the Apostle Philip, who was uniquely gifted in his way of preaching and teaching concerning the Kingdom of God through the name of Jesus. Men and women from all around came to hear about Jesus and were baptized. When you teach about the Kingdom of God and the name of Jesus Christ, others will be inspired. In addition, people will be amazed with your teaching and will also be amazed to see that miracles, signs, and wonders may be done around you.[3]

We must work as Kingdom citizens. As such, we are to bless our enemies as part of our character. Instead of being frustrated and angry with them, we must speak blessings. Our character should exude cheer. Having the character of God even means that we make friends with people we wouldn't normally make friends with.

Early in my career, I met a lady who talked about how a leader with character creates a rapport with others to make them comfortable dealing with you. She gave us tools and techniques to help us to develop a rapport with people whom we didn't know, even people who had come to the session from across the country. We were pressed to sit face to face with them and to get to know them by their spirit and their fruit, not necessarily by how they looked. We were encouraged to speak directly to the character that

God made in them, the people whom God made righteously, fearfully, and wonderfully through Christ Jesus. Through our own connection with God—our awareness that we are made new through His covenant—we can speak boldly to others about the ways of God.

Never Gives Up

The story in the Book of Daniel of the three Hebrew boys in the furnace has both spiritual and physical implications. Conventional wisdom would say that they should have given in to their oppressor's demand that they bow to a golden idol. After all, the threat had been pronounced that those who did not bow down would be thrown into the furnace. Thus, their physical lives were at stake. Their spiritual lives were also threatened because they knew that God had pronounced in ages past that no god was to be placed before Him. The Hebrew young men were willing to take the punishment of the furnace because they trusted God for deliverance. Of course, they were delivered.

Even when all indicators around them pointed to a disastrous end, the Hebrew young men didn't give up. People with Kingdom character don't give up. In your day-to-day life, you might see a situation that looks impossible, as if fire is surrounding you on every side so that you cannot see a way of escaping. This is a standard tactic that Satan uses to trick God's people into thinking that there is no way out, no way to success. However, as a person of Kingdom character, you will be able to recognize the situation for what it is—an opportunity to depend on God.

In such high-stakes situations, you can't be neutral in your response. The only effective response is to stand for and with God. If you give in to the pressures around you, the authority that you once had in God will be gone. You will lose the power that would have otherwise seen you through the tough times. If you want to be effective in God's Kingdom, you have to stand for Him. Don't give Satan any room to trick you. The result of the trick is to advance into your life more and more so that your life becomes chaotic and unrecognizable. Take a stand. Never give up.

Gives Cheerfully

Would you agree that God is a giver? I hope so. He is actually the *best* giver. He gave us our lives, our earthly home—and most important of all—His son. God is a giver. If we are to be people who live in God's image—people who have Kingdom character—then, we must give. Some people get distracted about the target of their giving. They might say, "I'm not giving to that church. I don't like the pastor." Someone might say, "I am not donating to that person. How do I know what he or she is doing with the money?" God instructs us in His Word that we are to give. It is that simple. When we give, we aren't giving to a church or to a particular organization or person. We are following the commandments of God and giving to His kingdom work. We are giving to Him. Anyway, God has a way of giving to the people He has instructed us to give to.

I have a friend who wasn't a consistent giver, but her fiancé was. Although he didn't have much money as a full-time student who worked part time, he faithfully paid his tithe. He also gave of his time to many people who needed help. Over time, my friend began to notice that unexpected checks would appear in the fiancé's mailbox. A church member from his home state would send him a check just because the church member thought of him. In another case, a woman in the church he had started attending while at school said that she was part of an organization that would give him a scholarship. The fiancé didn't have the best grades, so this was a clear sign that the scholarship was truly a gift from God.

My friend became a consistent giver because of the example set by the fiancé. God uses those of kingdom character to reach His people on His behalf. There is no need to worry about what you might miss by being a giver. Go ahead and give, and make sure that you do it cheerfully.

Dominates Territory and Destiny

God has given us dominion over all the earth, and as Jabez believed in his prayer in 1 Chronicles 4:10, I believe God will expand the territory of my influence and yours too. Think about where your area of influence is. There is some part of your life where you garner more attention than in others. Where is it that people really trust you more than any other? I am not suggesting that you have a reputation of being untrustworthy in other areas. However, where is it that you are particularly skilled and where others recognize your abilities? For instance, in just about every area of my life—my work as an engineer, my work as a pastor, and my work in community engagement—I am a leader. You picked up this book because you thought that I had some level of credibility in the area of leadership. It is in the area of leadership—in the territory over which I have been given God's authority—that I dominate. In this area, I can execute the Word of God against the evil that may be put in place to try to thwart God's Kingdom agenda. There is some domain over which God has given you authority. You, too, have the authority to speak God's Word of dominion over the territory. You speak this Word through the name of Jesus and the power of the Holy Spirit.

Almost everyone is familiar with two particular people who adopted character traits very unlike Kingdom character. You remember Adam and Eve, right? We know that the Book of Genesis tells of the dominion that God gave to Adam and the subsequent disobedience of Adam and Eve. Their disobedience was enough to show their loss of kingdom character, but look at what happened when they became aware of God's presence after the disobedient act:

"Then the man and his wife heard the sound of the LORD God as he was walking in the garden in the cool of the day, and they hid from the LORD God among the trees of the garden." (Genesis 3:8)

Would God hide? God is always present, and He makes His presence known. Adam and Eve "heard the sound of the Lord God." Because God is right where He is supposed to be, where He has dominion—which is everywhere—He has no reservations about letting others know that He is present. Leaders take full authority over their domain. Adam's decision to hide and to lead his wife in hiding was an indicator that he had lost his Kingdom character because God does not hide from anything. We are to lead as God leads. We are to dominate as God dominates.

One key component of Kingdom character is leadership. Even earthly kings understand, without a doubt, that they have to stand for their beliefs and actions. I like how The Message Bible puts it in Chapter 12 of Romans: "if you're put in charge, don't manipulate."

Opens His or Her Mind to Learn

Depending on where you are in your level of leadership, it might be difficult for you to envision that your way of thinking will be completely different when you develop Kingdom character, but it will. As we move forward to develop our character as Kingdom leaders, God will cause our thinking to be vastly different than before, and this will be done according to His purpose, His likeness, and His will. Through your new Kingdom character, you will see in your spirit that God has made it possible for you to do the impossible. You will reach places that you never thought you would be.

The process of achieving the impossible begins with God Himself. He shows us how to seek His Kingdom through His Word and his creation. With this also comes a requirement on our part that we recognize the Lordship of Jesus and God the Father and our seal of redemption that is the Holy Spirit. This process is the beginning of our minds opening up to new possibilities.

Maintains Merchant Mentality

God talks about the character of a man in Romans 12:1–19. Take some time now to look at your favorite translation of this passage in Romans. In this passage, we learn that God wants us to offer EVERYTHING to Him—our sleeping, eating, going to work, and even walking around. EVERYTHING.

I always like to encourage people. I used to go down to a particular area of town with a few dollars to buy newspapers from the people who sold them there, just to support them. I would give a dollar to one person, take the paper, and then go to the next person to buy a paper. There was one guy I would love to see. I would drive down a certain road just because I knew that I would see this guy. I would actually go out of my way. Some mornings, he would have the paper on the ground, he'd kneel on one knee, and he would have his hands raised. He would also wave at people as they passed.

One morning, I asked, "What are you doing? Why are you down on one knee?" He said, "Well, I'm praying to God." I said, "Why do you have your hands up, and why are you moving like that?" He responded, "Because that is how I worship Him." Sometimes, he would jump up and down. He would be there selling papers as if it was the most important thing in the world to do. He would do it in a way that had the kind of vigor and vitality that God wants from our character. He never acted as if he didn't need or want to be there. He would be there every day, no matter what, whether it was hot or cold. He wouldn't quit in hard times. He would praise even harder. God wants that from all of us. He wants us to offer Him EVERYTHING.

We all should be as determined as the worshiping newspaper salesman. The mentality of this merchant was that he had to be dedicated to his work in a way that pleased God. He offered his best. That is what God requires.

Commits

What Jesus did for us in his life's ministry before death, in death, and in his life after death shows a level of commitment to his people that most of us could hardly fathom. Can we bring ourselves to be this committed? Jesus's words tell us just what commitment is:

> "...*I am with you always, even to the very end of the age*" *(Matthew 28:20 NIV).*

Accepting responsibility to complete a task or to execute a program is serious. Some people are consumed with the idea of seeing their names next to impressive titles but appear to be little interested in doing the work that the title suggests. Still others are all in favor for the work while it is easy and without challenges. When personalities become difficult to manage or when the resources wane, they might decide that the adventure is over.

Kingdom character and commitment go together. A person with kingdom character commits because he or she knows the stakes. This person commits in the first place because of the clear awareness that he or she has been called to a certain vision to dominate a certain territory. It is your destiny to dominate, and domination calls for tenacity. So, it is not just that you are helping out or doing something nice. When you tap into the concept of kingdom character, you know that you commit only to those things that God has called you to.

Have you committed to God's vision for your life? Will you take your cues from Jesus? Will you be with God's plan until "the very end of the age"? Can God count on you?

Humbles Himself or Herself

With a book title that includes "Power Principles," one might think that humility would have no place in the discussion. Humility might seem at first glance to be the antithesis of power. However, we need only to think about our ultimate example of power, Jesus, in order to understand that humility is a necessary vehicle to power. Consider these words from Matthew 16: 24:

"Then, Jesus said to His disciples, "Whoever wants to be my disciple must deny themselves and take up their cross and follow me." (Matthew 16:24)

In order to gain access to Jesus's power, the disciples had to be humble. They had to suppress their priorities and follow Jesus's lead.

From the *Kingdom Character* book:

"Being humble is knowing who is resident Owner and Lord in our lives and bowing down to Him as King. God is always the Boss. Some of us have the wrong boss—we choose others and even ourselves over God. It is God who fuels us day to day. He ignites us and lifts us to higher heights to Him. Seek more grace by being humble, and God will elevate you in due season."[4]

Aligns Thoughts with High Altitude

I have thought long and hard about this concept of being above the crowd, being at a high altitude. As believers in Christ, our thinking should be so elevated that we realize that we are sitting in heavenly places and "are able to be lifted above our situations and problems to a heavenly sphere with Christ Jesus as our Head."[5]

Getting to such a high altitude isn't the easiest thing to do. As we aim for Kingdom character, let us consider what we are putting inside of us. Only when we breathe in what is of God can our actions represent the kind of character that God has. Our culture has plenty of practices that can shape us into its image. Think about the latest TV show that is leading the market. Think about the music that is at the top of the charts. Consider how people spend their time, in ways that are said to be harmless. But are they of God?

Consider these words from my book *Kingdom Character*:

"Always walk away from anything that is counterfeit or contrary to the Word of God. When you walk in the Spirit, the Holy Spirit will guide you to a better way. Management of our lifestyle is paramount in the Kingdom of God. Our life has a style or sway (level of influence). What sway does your life have? Is your life governed by the ways of God or the ways of the world? Which voice do you listen to daily—God's, the enemy's, yours, or reason?"

Once God has breathed into us, we have a connection that we have never had before. Unlike those people who are around us who can potentially cause a weight or drag on us, God lifts us and causes us to excel. With Him, we have momentum in our lives. He takes us to different levels of maturity in our character. He may cause us to be more assertive and directional or maybe even more organized or meek. He brings us to a place of maturity where we can have a well-formed Kingdom life that brings out the best in us. When God speaks and breathes into us, we are led to do what God says.

A person of Kingdom character is a person whose mind is totally focused on the work of God. This person is led by faith and goes wherever God calls. If you are a person of kingdom character, you are allowing God to mold your thinking, which means that you are thinking big and dreaming big and that you are on your special path. God has given you gifts so that you can walk a path specially designed for you. When we walk this ordained path, we and others can clearly see what God is doing.

One way to align our thoughts with the high altitude of God is to really watch our associations with others. If you hang out with people who are not following the Word of God, you could be negatively influenced by them. Be careful in that regard. Either you are influencing them or they are influencing you! There is usually no middle ground. Time will tell who wins. The animal you feed wins. Manage your style by staying away from any suspicious activity.

Knowing my priorities helps me to keep my thoughts in the elevated place where they should be. Adam and Eve show us the dangers of losing your sense of order. In order for Kingdom character to be present, a sense of order has to be present as well. Both Adam and Eve knew that God was the source of all knowledge, yet they deviated from this order to follow what felt or sounded right. They traded the best thing (the Garden of Eden) for what *seemed* like the best thing (the fruit). Did you get that? They traded a whole garden for one piece of fruit! Even today when someone is attempting to give the best description of a beautiful natural environment, the person might say that it is a "Garden of Eden." It was God's best, the ideal environment for God's people. It was even fit for God to walk in the cool of the day. However, in order for Adam and Eve to continue to dwell in such a grand place, in the place where God walked, they had to follow God's order. The same is true for us now.

If we are to achieve mighty feats, we must see ourselves in the high place where God walks. This simply means that we must maintain the vision for our lives that God has for us, but what does living in vision look like?

Those with this component of Kingdom character worship and praise with enthusiasm, even in rough times. They understand that their particular tone will set the tone for people around them. As leaders, they know that their tone will create an accumulation of awesome fruit in their lives. They see this in their vision. They know that their thoughts have the power to create a physical reality.

Repents

To repent simply means to turn away from sin. In the Bible, John the Baptist called out for people to repent. Jesus followed with the same message:

> *". . . Repent, for the kingdom of heaven has come near." (Matthew 4:17, NIV)*

This Scripture plainly argues that sin and the Kingdom cannot coexist. Furthermore, it suggests that there is a moment of division between what you might have done before and the possibilities that are in your future if you sever previous negative behaviors from your life.

Let's be honest—we have all done something that we aren't particularly proud of. But, you can decide today to be a person of Kingdom character, leaving behind manipulation of others so that you can get ahead, misusing resources that you have charge of, and dismissing the needs of others who work with you. You can be a different kind of person, a person who is more concerned with the Kingdom of God than the offerings of men.

Aligns Strategically with Your Purpose

God uniquely made each of us for a particular purpose, and He gave us our experiences for the following reasons:

1. To know that Jesus is Lord, and that every knee and everything with a name shall bow to Him.
2. Because it was in His plan for us to have the best path to find Him.
3. So that we could be sure that He is the One doing it for us and through us.
4. To know Him in diverse ways.
5. To remember that He, and He alone, is God.
6. To build His Kingdom and tear down Satan's counterfeit kingdom.
7. To make Him known throughout the world as the great commission mandates.

"God calls us to be ministers of His gospel, to be committed to the Word of reconciliation, to follow Christ as His ambassadors, and to bear fruit that will remain for His Kingdom. Your purpose is to be in alignment with His Word and to make Him known. Your destiny will always lead to Christ. Your strategy should be to align yourself with the Word of God, pray, study, and fast and within time your purposed destiny will emerge."[6]

We might wonder about the purpose of encountering obstacles along our journey. It would seem that if we just make the right decisions that our course will be smooth sailing. However, know that even if you have the Kingdom character necessary to make the right choices that disorder, disharmony, and disunity can still present themselves. With Kingdom character already in place, you will be able to understand the purpose of these unwelcomed guests. If you are a person of Kingdom character, the unwelcomed guests will visit only for the ultimate goal of your life's purpose.

Understand that they are somehow linked with your purpose and that spiritual intelligence will emerge. You will gain some level of insight into your next leadership move. Paying the price of confronting disorder, disharmony, and disunity is sometimes necessary to create the powerful, explosive, and creative movement that will further God's agenda. Take heart that the direction and purpose that God has for your life is still on course.

After your encounter, you will be ready to become the person God has called you to be. You will be ready to enter the higher place in God that requires you to be stronger than ever. Instead of walking in a place where you will be distracted by menial things where your thoughts will waver from your purpose, you will have the kind of clarity that will allow you to walk with God in the cool of the day regardless of the forces that attempt to come against you and the challenges that you may face.

The evidence of Kingdom character is in the choices that we make. Likewise, we have to make certain kinds of choices in order to have Kingdom character. It is really a cycle. Let me explain. For instance, we must keep our minds and bodies intact in order to demonstrate Kingdom character. We have to have the right fuel (food) that will provide the balance that we need to make decisions that reflect character. We have to have the best thoughts.

"Finally, brothers and sisters, whatever is true, whatever is noble, whatever is right, whatever is pure, whatever is lovely, whatever is admirable—if anything is excellent or praiseworthy—think about such things." (Philippians 4:8)

To fulfill the loop, we must have the character necessary to make these kinds of choices. If I don't have my mind made up that I am going to make kingdom choices, I can easily choose the fries on the menu instead of the baked potato.

There is no doubt that you were created for God's purpose. Chapter 12 of 1 Corinthians shows us that we are part of the body of Christ. Anyone who has taken a moment to think about how amazing the human body is can appreciate this passage in 1 Corinthians. Just as the hand serves the purposes of the human body, people of Kingdom character serve the body of Christ. Hands are specifically designed to pick up things. There is no other body part that can do a better job. Likewise, we are fashioned to serve God in a particular way that is just as excellent and just as miraculous as the hand. How can you contribute to the body of Christ in the special way that God has designed you?

This question is bigger than you might think. God is calling you to work with people who don't have the same skills that you have in your character. (If you are a hand, they might be the arm or leg.) It can be frustrating, even irritating, to work with them. Remember the example of the beach ball and how God breathes into you and shapes you? Because love is a part of your character—since God breathed it into you—keep a smile on your face when people present who they are. Just keep working and walking in God's purpose for you.

Cultivates Your Full Range

Fully actualizing your Kingdom character is the opposite of living a comfortable life. Without a Kingdom view of life, we can see only a sliver of our potential. I like how Apostle

Paul puts it. This time, I will use the King James Version because I think it paints the picture so nicely:

"For now we see through a glass, darkly; but then face to face: now I know in part; but then shall I know even as also I am known." (1 Corinthians 13: 12, KJV)

Without a Kingdom view, we are like someone who looks into a dark mirror. We are unable to see the full image, only hints of it. With a Kingdom view, we will be able to see ourselves fully, as God sees us—"then shall I know even as also I am known." As people of Kingdom character, we must operate in the way that God sees us. We cannot be limited by our own limited view.

Perhaps, my words from my Kingdom Character book will help to expound on this concept:

"To cultivate our full range, we should seek the Holy Spirit on a daily basis to reveal to us what is on God's mind for us. Developing our full range will cause us to leave our comfort zones and arcs of safety to move in the anointing that God has placed in our care. When we develop our full ranges, we will see miracles, signs, and wonders happen around us. When we develop our full ranges, we may be asked to move to another city, start new ministries, or venture out to do things we never imagined doing before.

Paul taught Timothy to develop his full range in preaching. He encouraged young Timothy to preach the Word no matter what—in season or out of season, whether they wanted to hear him or not, when he was popular or unpopular, and when he felt like it or even did not feel like it.

Don't pull back; it is part of your appointment to bear fruit for Christ—fruit that will remain. If God calls you to bear fruit by moving across the country or to another part of the world, will you be ready?[7]

Takes Action

"You should take every opportunity to tell your stories to people as a witness to the goodness of God."[8]

We connect with each other through the telling of our stories. This, in itself, is action. When I tell my story of receiving God's vision for my life, I am taking action. I cannot underestimate the power of telling your story. We know of certain significant figures in history because of the stories of their lives. How much better is it to know about how God's goodness has brought about a triumph in a person's life. Sharing this kind of story helps people to connect with God's vision for them. If God can have a vision for you, certainly He has one for the next person. Therefore, you must share your God-inspired story whenever you can. It has power.

Endures

"Our world economy is going through so much unrest these days. So many people have been laid off their jobs, and finding employment continues to be a challenge for so many. As more than conquerors, we must stay strong and endure through these times and look for Jesus to bring us out.

One of my co-workers encourages me to endure through my new exercise regimen. When he sees me in the hall at work, he always asks how my exercise routine is going. His questions are quite probing to ensure that I am enduring the changes in lifestyle. He suggested that for me to endure, I should take the marathoner's course of action, developing strong, lean muscles for distance. His recommendation included less weight, more repetitions, and more sets. He said that this would help me to be strong and endure. "Endurance through more repetitions and more sets in life will build kingly character and enable you to endure."[9]

Risks for the Kingdom

Simply having character means that you have what it takes to stand against pressure. This is even more so with Kingdom character. It is always a risk to do what is right in the face of conflict. However, it is the ultimate risk to take a stand for an issue that will build the Kingdom of God. I wrote about this issue in my Kingdom Character book:

"Taking a risk means that many times we should take a stand for something to build the Kingdom and possibly to save a life for the Kingdom. In Esther's case [Esther 4:13-17], she was saving a nation from imminent danger from a longstanding enemy, Hamon. Hamon stood for evil, and evil alone, against the nation of Israel. His intent was to annihilate the Jews from the face of the earth. Esther was asked by Mordecai (her relative who raised her from a child) to take a risk by going to the king uninvited to save the nation. It was unheard of for a person to go before a king uninvited. Esther took the risk and bowed before the king with her request for dinner (banquet), and she used this time to talk about the fate of her nation.

We should take risks for the Kingdom today. Integrity is needed today. Speak up for your brother or sister in the right way and time when they are being treated harshly. Speak up for Jesus with boldness."[10]

Thoughts for Kingdom Character

In the space below, list some additional reflections you have about the type of Kingdom character you would like to have in your relationship with God.

Chapter 6
Transforming You—Power Reinstated

Transforming You

At the beginning of the last chapter, we looked at how man's character stacked up against God's in the Garden of Eden. We all know how that scenario ended.

> *"So the LORD God banished him from the Garden of Eden to work the ground from which he had been taken." (Genesis 3:23)*

Adam and Eve had begun to hide from God, and once this happened, a transformation was in order. Ultimately, man had to be redeemed and transformed, and the land had to be restored back to him.

Even with the Fall of man, God had always planned for his people to be renewed. The first step to restoration is renewal. When we accept Christ as Savior and desire to be conformed to His character and nature, then our character is destined to change. When we find ourselves with the same kind of thinking that is prevalent in our society, we are in need of renewal. Leadership is one of those areas wrought with the kind of thinking that is counter to the concepts of Kingdom leadership. Thus, anyone seeking the benefits of Kingdom citizenship and kingship must be willing to also be transformed. The Scripture notes how our way of thinking, and, thus, our character, will be renewed.

> **"And do not be conformed to this world, but be transformed by the renewing of your mind, that you may prove what is that good and acceptable and perfect will of God." (Romans 12:2)**

This transformation is tantamount to a type of spiritual metamorphosis. While a physical metamorphosis connotes a change in our outward appearance, we should actually be outwardly demonstrating our inner redeemed natures on a daily basis. This only comes as the Holy Spirit starts to change the way we think and as we clothe ourselves daily in the Word of God.

We have already been created in the image and likeness of God, and the goal of this transformation is that we would become like Christ in character, to live for the things that are unseen, to live by the Spirit, and to be yielded to God.[1]

We achieve this transformation as we allow the Holy Spirit who is in us to control our souls and bodies. God has given us the (dunamis), miracle-working power of His Holy Spirit. This is the same power that Jesus used when He ministered here on earth (see Acts 1:8). This gives us the ability to do all things through Christ because He is the One who strengthens us (see Philippians 4:13).

There are two things to bear in mind about this transformation.

1. <u>Transformation is a daily process.</u> It will not happen all at once. We are continually being transformed into His likeness. We spend a lifetime learning how to live by the Spirit and how to live a new life. We are required to 'work out' our salvation with fear and trembling. We have to continually submit to God—taking every thought captive to make it obedient to Christ (practicing a Kingdom mindset).
2. <u>We cannot do it alone.</u> We do this Kingdom work in cooperation with God. We are His fellow workers, in His field; we are His building (see 1 Corinthians 3:9).

"For it is God who works in you both to will and to do for His good pleasure." (Philippians 2:13)

We work and God works; we labor together. We have the responsibility to work and to be God's representatives in this earth realm. He actually produces the good works and spiritual fruit in us through the indwelling of the Holy Spirit. It is the power of God that makes us willing and gives us the motivation to want to live transformed lives. Doing so for His good pleasure simply means He desires that we choose to do that which satisfies Him. He wants us to want Him and to want what He wants for us.

Our part in this transformation work doesn't occur by simply willing it to be so. We cannot do it by ourselves. A farmer cannot cause his crops to grow. What he can do is create conditions favorable for growth and protect his crops from parasites, diseases, and other forces that seek to destroy his crops. In the same way, we cannot cause God's character to grow within us–He is the only One capable of doing that. We can, however, create favorable conditions for growth—through faith, prayer, and study of the Word of God.

The Word of God teaches that He has provided for us a new heart, mind, spirit, nature, and ultimately a new name.[2]

We are truly transformed.

Our part in this labor includes

1. Believing that God can and will transform us into His image.
2. Choosing to be transformed, choosing to live by the Spirit, choosing to submit to God, and choosing to be a weapon of righteousness.
3. Staying in the Word; this is the agent that renews and transforms the mind.
4. Guarding our thoughts daily by thinking on things that are true, noble, just, pure, lovely, of good report, that have virtue, and are praiseworthy (Philippians 4:8).[3]

Power Reinstated

As mentioned previously, God's plan has always been to restore dominion power to his people. In the book of Zechariah, that restoration is given through His love for the chosen people of Israel after their many years of oppression. The restoration of their relationship also included the reinstatement of their authority and power. Not only would their temple be rebuilt, but the city itself would also expand due to its restored prosperity, as seen in Isaiah 40:9-10. All of this is to be completely fulfilled in the millennial Kingdom of the Messiah (see Revelation 20).

> *"'I am jealous for Jerusalem and for Zion with great jealousy. I am exceedingly angry with the nations at ease; for I was a little angry, and they helped—but with evil intent'. Therefore thus says the LORD: 'I am returning to Jerusalem with mercy; My house shall be built in it,' says the LORD of hosts, 'and a surveyor's line shall be stretched out over Jerusalem.' Again proclaim, saying, 'thus says the LORD of hosts: 'My cities shall again spread out through prosperity; The LORD will again comfort Zion, and will again choose Jerusalem.'" (Zechariah 1:14b-17)*

As previously discussed, the first thing that God did after creating the heavens and the earth was to make man and give him governing authority and dominion over the earth realm. God created the earth with the intent that man should own it and live on it. Man's Fall resulted in having that governing authority temporarily taken from him, but it was later restored after the sacrificial death of Christ Jesus on the cross. That governing authority will be fully realized with the consummation of the redeemed bride in the New Jerusalem.

> *"Then I saw a new heaven and a new earth, for the first heaven and the first earth had passed away. ... And I heard a loud voice from the throne saying, 'Now the dwelling of God is with men, and He will live with them. They will be His people, and God Himself will be with them and be their God. ... for the old order of things has passed away.' He who was seated on the throne said, 'I am making everything new!'"*
> *(Revelation 21:1, 3, 4b-5a)*

Those who are followers and true believers of Christ will have the opportunity to share in reigning with Him as His bride. In order to do so, we have a responsibility as His followers to be hearers and doers of His Word. The purpose of the Word was so that our lives could be transformed. It provides life and nourishment, while also providing instruction and conviction.

"All Scripture is inspired by God and is useful to teach us what is true and to make us realize what is wrong in our lives. It corrects us when we are wrong and teaches us to do what is right. God uses it to prepare and equip His people to do every good work."
(2 Timothy 3:16-17 NIV)

The Word of God is essential for a transformed life. God gave us the living Word—Jesus—to be the author and finisher of our faith. He, then, provided the written Word to prepare us for living out our faith.

In order to fulfill the purpose and calling that God has placed upon us, we must come to terms with who we really are—inside and out. That which we are, we will do.

"For as he thinks in his heart, so is he." *(Proverbs 23:7a)*

Transformation requires that we become like the inner being of Christ Himself. We must become the types of people who routinely and easily walk in the goodness and power of Christ. To the degree that a spiritual transformation to inner Christlikeness is successful, our outer lives will transform into a natural expression of the character and teachings of Jesus. That which God has equipped and prepared us to do will manifest and we will be able to "walk the walk."

Our efforts must be based upon an understanding of the Word of God. John 15:5 lets us know that we can do nothing without Christ. We succeed in the transformation process by finding ways to continually abiding in Him (see John 15:1-7). Those ways can be illustrated through maintaining Kingdom Vision, Intention, and Means.

- Vision of life in the Kingdom: Christ's vision is clearly stated; He came for one purpose—*"I must preach the kingdom of God." (Luke 4:43)*
- Intentionally being Kingdom-Minded: Intentionally deciding to live in the Kingdom as Christ lived, and being obedient to His Word and commandments.
- Means for Spiritual Transformation: Replacing the 'lost' person with the inner character of Christ through such things as study and meditation of His Word, prayer, and fellowship and accountability to others.

As mentioned previously, God's plan has always been to restore dominion power to his people.

The LORD's Plan

"In that day," declares the LORD, "I will gather the lame; I will assemble the exiles and those I have brought to grief. I will make the lame my remnant, those driven away a strong nation. The LORD will rule over them in Mount Zion from that day and forever. As for you, watchtower of the flock, stronghold of Daughter Zion, the former dominion will be restored to you; kingship will come to Daughter Jerusalem."
(Micah 4:6-8)

Thoughts for Transforming You–Power Reinstated:

In the space below, list some additional reflections you have about your transformation and your reinstated power to have dominion and authority as God's representative. List the ways you will begin achieving this transformation.

Chapter 7
Kingdom Atmosphere

An atmosphere is a mood of a place. If we are in a magnificent ballroom with glistening chandeliers and tables set with linen and silver, we say that the atmosphere is a formal one. If we are at a beach reclining on the sand and listening to the waves of the ocean brush against the shore, we say that the atmosphere is relaxing. Certain components are present in certain kinds of atmospheres. Just as we can act to create a formal or relaxing atmosphere, we can act to create a Kingdom atmosphere. But first, let's explore what we mean by *Kingdom atmosphere*.

> **"But God, who is rich in mercy, because of His great love with which He loved us, even when we were dead in trespasses, made us alive together with Christ (by grace you have been saved), and raised us up together, and made us sit together in heavenly places in Christ Jesus." (Ephesians 2:4-6)**

Our rightful context is in the heavenly places, the ultimate Kingdom atmosphere. By God's great mercy, grace, and love, we are not only dead to sin, but we are also alive to righteousness through the resurrection of Christ. What is even more extraordinary, is the fact that we share His pre-eminent glory. We are invited to sit together in His glory in the heavenly places.

As the process of transformation occurs, and with the understanding that we are seated together with Christ in heavenly places, our thinking must move higher. If you received an invitation from the White House to attend a dinner where you would be among the world's leaders, would you think of yourself at a higher level than before you received the invitation? Our heavenly invitation is even better. Unlike the White House dinner, the heavenly banquet doesn't call for the best dress or tuxedo to cover our bodies. Preparation for the heavenly table requires inward, spiritual preparation. This preparation is all a part of establishing the Kingdom atmosphere. We have been granted an extraordinary invitation to be the representatives of God in this earth realm. It is here that we are to establish a Kingdom atmosphere.

Even when the atmosphere is not aligned with this higher existence, we have the ability to change the atmosphere because we are equipped with the weapons of spiritual warfare. God responds to certain sounds that are released toward heaven. The sound of prayer and the atmosphere of worship have the ability to cause miraculous things to occur. Operating within a Kingdom atmosphere requires that we not function according to the flesh but live in the Spirit, and prayer and worship are our tools for living in the Spirit. Below is an example of how believers created a Kingdom atmosphere with their prayer and worship.

"But at midnight Paul and Silas were praying and singing hymns to God, and the prisoners were listening

> *to them. Suddenly there was a great earthquake, so that the foundations of the prison were shaken; and immediately all the doors were opened and everyone's chains were loosed. And the keeper of the prison, awaking from sleep and seeing the prison doors open, supposing the prisoners had fled, drew his sword and was about to kill himself. But Paul called with a loud voice, saying, 'Do yourself no harm, for we are all here'. Then he called for a light, ran in, and fell down trembling before Paul and Silas, and he brought them out and said, 'Sirs, what must I do to be saved?'"*
> *(Acts 16:25-29)*

The Kingdom atmosphere that Paul and Silas set with prayers and hymns clearly prepared the way for the miracle of their freedom. Actually, the release of their chains did not constitute the entire miracle. This passage is packed full of miracles. It was also miraculous that Paul and Silas did not run when their chains were loosed. Because they stayed, they were able to speak life into the guard so that the guard asked how he could be saved. The ultimate miracle was that Paul and Silas were instrumental in leading the guard to eternal salvation.

The lesson in this is that we have the ability to exercise Kingdom authority and establish a Kingdom atmosphere as long as the Lord is in the forefront. Our representation of God should never lead us to think that we can operate autonomously. God is always to be recognized as our source and our strength.

Some people seem to think that a Kingdom atmosphere can be created only in a traditional church setting. Paul and Silas show us that it can be created in the lowest of places, a jail. A Kingdom atmosphere can also be created so that we walk daily in it. We can pray and worship all day, whether at school or at work. You might be thinking that, in the United States, there are laws against religious activity in public schools and in most places of work. Even if the rules of your organization prohibit you from organizing a public religious activity like a prayer meeting, you can sing and pray as you go about your day. Is there someone stopping you from singing praise music on the way to work or praying softly as you walk from building to building on your campus? We can offer our very work as acts of worship. In Chapter 5, we discussed how we are to guard our thoughts daily by thinking on things that are true, noble, just, pure, lovely, of good report, that have virtue, and are praiseworthy (Philippians 4:8). By viewing our work as our worship, we can create a Kingdom atmosphere that creates our success.

Some elements of life have no place in a Kingdom atmosphere. In fact, their presence will make the creation of a Kingdom atmosphere impossible.

"For even if there are so-called gods, whether in heaven or on earth (as there are many gods and many lords), yet for us there is one God, the Father, of whom are all things, and we for Him; and one Lord Jesus Christ, through whom are all things, and through whom we live." (1 Corinthians 8:5-6)

There is only one true and living God, and we are commanded to place no other gods before Him. The culture that we live in places emphasis on many things as being a necessity for our everyday living—certain fashions, a house in a certain neighborhood, affiliations with certain people. However, these things, when used in an improper context may have the potential of becoming gods to us. It has to be clear that our Kingdom atmosphere should be filled with the presence of the one true God. He is the source of power and strength, and as long as He is in the forefront, we are assured of success and prosperity.

To continue to operate in an environment with *so-called gods* is to reject God's invitation to sit together in heavenly place, to live in a Kingdom atmosphere.

"So then, those who are in the flesh cannot please God. But you are not in the flesh but in the Spirit, if indeed the Spirit of God dwells in you. Now if anyone does not have the Spirit of Christ, he is not His. And if Christ is in you, the body is dead because of sin, but the Spirit is life because of righteousness."
(Romans 8:8-10)

Rejecting God's invitation is equal to choosing to dwell in the kingdom of darkness. And if you are living in the kingdom of darkness, you are a slave to the enemy Satan. A slave is one who is completely subject to another—whether it be slave to a habit or to an influence. Anything he controls, he also destroys.

These two kingdoms, the Kingdom of God and the kingdom of darkness, have totally different agendas, and with different destinations that will bring about different lifestyles. On earth, your life will be subject to someone's rule; it will either be the rule of God or the rule of Satan.

An atmosphere is the space around you, the space you inhabit. Be sure that the space that you are in is a Kingdom atmosphere. As God's representatives, and along with Him, we are always dwelling in His Kingdom. However, we must work diligently to maintain the Kingdom atmosphere by praying and worshiping. Even when you encounter spaces that are counter to what you know as God's dwelling place, change the atmosphere with your prayer and worship. The higher level of the Kingdom atmosphere has the power to break bonds, as Paul and Silas experienced.

Thoughts for Kingdom Atmosphere:

In the space below, list some additional reflections you have about Kingdom atmosphere. How will you be able to establish a Kingdom atmosphere in places where you interact with others—at home, at your workplace, or in your surrounding community of friends and neighbors?

Chapter 8
Keys to the Kingdom-Unlimited Access

"When Jesus came into the region of Caesarea Philippi, He asked His disciples, saying, 'Who do men say that I, the Son of Man, am?'...Simon Peter answered and said, 'You are the Christ, the Son of the living God.' Jesus answered and said to him, 'Blessed are you, Simon Bar-Jonah, for flesh and blood has not revealed this to you, but My Father who is in heaven. And I also say to you that you are Peter, and on this rock I will build My church, and the gates of Hades shall not prevail against it. And I will give you the keys of the kingdom of heaven, and whatever you bind on earth shall be bound in heaven, and whatever you loose on earth will loosed in heaven.'" (Matthew 16:13, 16-19)

The goal we want to reach in knowing the keys to the Kingdom secrets is to be able to declare, "I will never again have to say, 'All I have is...'"

Keys, simply stated, are used to lock and unlock doors. In this instance, God has given us the authority to lock and unlock the keys to the Kingdom of Heaven. Jesus was giving his disciples the authority to open the door to the Kingdom. It is through this door that one has the ability to enter into God's Kingdom. Jesus was laying the foundation for His Church, and the disciples were to be His representatives and lead the way. The disciples had the responsibility to represent Christ, as do we, as they went forth preaching the gospel. All those who respond in faith and repentance are granted access to the Kingdom.

The critical point that should be made is that one may only "enter" into the Kingdom by one means—there must be a spiritual transformation or regeneration that is produced by the Holy Spirit. As Jesus said,

"Most assuredly, I say to you, unless one is born again, he cannot see the kingdom of God." (John 3:3)

Jesus was speaking to Nicodemus and explaining to him that one has to be born again. This happens as the Holy Spirit works through the Word of God to bring about a new life in a dead sinner, the transformation process discussed in Chapter 6. Without faith and without being born again, the door to heaven is shut and restricted.

Keys can only unlock doors if they are the right keys. I amplified this situation in one of my previous books:

"Have you ever found some old keys lying around your house and couldn't remember what they were for? Possessing a key you cannot identify or match to a particular lock is as bad as not having any key at all. What good are keys that you can't use? They are as useless as locks you can't open."[1]

The Word of God provides us with all the tools and information we need to open every door, but even though we have all the information and power we need, most of us lack the knowledge in how to apply it. However, there are those whose hearts remain hardened and reject the gospel of Christ and His saving grace. They are excluded from the Kingdom. Moreover, those who possess the keys of knowledge and also hinder or bar entrance to others and prevent them from coming in, receive God's judgment.

"'Woe to you lawyers! For you have taken away the key of knowledge. You did not enter in yourselves, and those who were entering in you hindered.'"
(Luke 11:52)

"But woe to you, scribes and Pharisees, hypocrites! For you shut up the kingdom of heaven against men; for you neither go in yourselves, nor do you allow those who are entering to go in." (Matthew 23:13)

The Pharisees had rejected God's righteousness and sought to establish their own, and they also encouraged others to do the same. As a result, they were admonished because their legalism caused others to be blocked from the entrance into the Kingdom.

Your gifts and talents are the tools that should be used to further His plans. Along with the Word of God, they are to be used to unlock the doors that will release that purpose. Our life and authority in the Kingdom requires resuming our God-given governing authority in the earth realm and learning how to live and function within that authority. We have to know how to use the keys of the Kingdom.

"And He said, 'To you it has been given to know the mysteries of the kingdom of God..." (Luke 8:10a)

Understanding the spiritual truths of the Kingdom is a gracious gift freely and sovereignly granted only to God's representatives. Those who are not of God are disregarded and passed over. These are the ones who reap the natural results of their own lack of faith and rebellion.

Thoughts for the Keys of the Kingdom—Unlimited Access

In the space below, list some additional thoughts that you have about using the keys of the Kingdom and having unlimited access. Discuss how you will be using your gifts and talents as keys to unlock doors in your home, in your community, at your place of employment, or in any other area that may be your sphere of influence.

Chapter 9
Governing Influence

By this point, the transformation of our thinking should have propelled us to the place where we now fully understand that there has to be a shift in our thinking. We cannot continue as members of a tolerant audience, as so many members of a church do. Instead, we must be active members of a unified army. We should not be content to remain spectators, but be compelled to become active participants in the Kingdom move of God.

It is time for us to embrace the reality that Kingdom leaders have governing influence. This means that we are in charge and that we impact others with the choices that we make. The solutions to a Kingdom community's needs must be found within those who are in strategic positions of influence within the Kingdom of God. The center of influence within that Kingdom is our Lord, and He has given His representatives the authority to govern on His behalf.

Our ability to influentially govern using the authority given by God should create a demand for the knowledge of the keys of the Kingdom. The people who need to return to God should be attracted to the special attribute of governing influence that God has placed in His Kingdom leaders. If you are a Kingdom leader, people will be drawn to you because of the special role that God has designated to you.

The presence of governing influence is evidence of a strong spiritual connection with the Lord for He is the One who is the central component. Spiritual connection comes from seeking and listening to the voice of the Lord. Through this extended spiritual connection, God elevates his people to have governing influence:

"Now it shall come to pass, if you diligently obey the voice of the LORD your God, to observe carefully all His commandments which I commanded you today, that the LORD your God will set you high above all nations of the earth. And all these blessings shall come upon you and overtake you, because you obey the voice of the LORD your God." (Deuteronomy 28:1-2)

With your elevation by God comes blessings. The Word of God also tells us that blessings are a result of unity. The beauty about Kingdom work is that it is designed to be accomplished in connection with others. The key principle in the Kingdom is that where there is unity, God is in the midst commanding blessings. These blessings will manifest under the unity of the anointing.

"Behold, how good and how pleasant it is for brethren to dwell together in unity! It is like the precious ointment poured on the head, that ran down on the beard, even the beard of Aaron [the high priest], that came down upon the collar and skirts of his garments [consecrating the whole body]. It is like the dew of

[lofty] Mount Hermon and the dew that comes on the hills of Zion; for there the Lord has commanded the blessing, even life forevermore [upon the high and the lofty]." (Psalm 133:1-3 AMP)

The full blessings of God stem from total obedience to His Word. Those who are obediently positioned under the anointing, unified, and one with God are the recipients of those blessings.

The Power of Unity

God only breathes on that which is connected. Being unified and one with God places us under the power of the anointing and solidifies our authority in the Kingdom. This is all done through the power of the Trinity. Just as the three essences of the chemical H_2O are found in water, steam, and ice, then the three essences of God are found in the Trinity—the Father, the Son, and the Holy Spirit. They are all One and the same, and where there is one, there is unity. In fact, unity is powerful even when it is not focused on God's plan, as the Scripture below shows:

"And they said, 'Come, let us build ourselves a city, and a tower whose top is in the heaven; let us make a name for ourselves, lest we be scattered abroad over the face of the whole earth.' But the LORD came down to see the city and the tower which the sons of men had built. And the LORD said, 'Indeed the people are one and they all have one language, and this is what they begin to do; now nothing that they propose to do will be withheld from them.'" (Genesis 11:4-6)

Unfortunately for these people, instead of receiving God's blessing, they received His judgment due to their wrong motives. However, the principle of "one" fully operates within the earth realm. Their governing influence was fully operational. They understood the principle of unity in the Kingdom. The Lord was also aware of this power of unity, and, therefore, stated that there was nothing that would be withheld from them.

The good news is that unity does work for the benefit of God's people as well, in accordance with His plan and direction:

> *"And the LORD said to Joshua: 'See! I have given Jericho into your hand, its king, and the mighty men of valor. You shall march around the city, all you men of war; you shall go around the city once. This you shall do six days. The seven priests shall bear seven trumpets of rams' horns before the ark. But the seventh day you shall march around the city seven times, and the priests shall blow the trumpets. It shall come to pass, when they make a long blast of the ram's horn, and when you hear the sound of the trumpet, that all the people shall shout with a great shout; then the wall of the city shall fall down flat.' ...So the people shouted when the priests blew the trumpets. And it happened when the people heard the sound of the trumpet, and the people shouted with a great shout, that the wall fell down flat." (Joshua 6:2-5a, 20a)*

Their shout in unison conveyed an expectation of God's prevailing action to fulfill His guaranteed promise, and their unified voice brought down the walls of the city. God often calls an influencer to unite His people for His purposes. Your governing influence and victory in every situation totally depends on the ability to be one and unified within the Kingdom, just as God is One with the Trinity. With a unified body operating in the will of God—that is, one people with one voice—nothing is withheld.

In the last example, Joshua served in this capacity. Everyone is influenced by something or someone. It is important to be influenced according to the plan that God has for you, so stay connected with Him through prayer and the reading of His Word so that you are influenced for the purpose of Kingdom building.

How Do You Influence?

Joshua was a great leader and was able to lead the people of God to victory. They trusted in his influence and faith in God. A prime example of an influencer in today's American political culture is the political lobbyist. Lobbyists exist at every level of government and are individuals who may be paid to be advocates in areas of special interests. Lobbyists depend on cultivating personal relationships over a period of time. After cultivating these relationships, they are often in strategic positions to influence decision making by promoting the special interests of those who employ them.

Influence works differently in the body of Christ. Within the body of Christ, there are certain areas of influence that represent the five-fold ministry giftings of the church:[1]

1. Apostles – govern
2. Prophets – guide
3. Evangelists – gather
4. Pastors – guard
5. Teachers – ground

"And He Himself gave some to be apostles, some prophets, some evangelists, and some pastors and

teachers for the equipping of the saints for the work of ministry, for the edifying of the body of Christ, till we all come to the unity of the faith and of the knowledge of the Son of God, to a perfect man, to the measure of the stature of the fullness of Christ."
(Ephesians 4:11-13)

God has set his representatives in places of influence for His church to function and for the Kingdom to be developed. Those truly called into these places will have been tested and proven, having gone through the fire of preparation, and they will display true humility and Christ-likeness, not desiring a position or office, but wanting only to serve their King in any way He desires to be served.

Each office is described below:

Apostle
An apostle is one who is called and sent by God to have spiritual authority, character, gifts, and abilities to reach and establish people in Kingdom truth and order, especially through founding and overseeing local churches. An apostle has a burden to build something that didn't exist before. They lay the foundation of new local churches and see to it that they come into full maturity.

Prophet
Prophets reveal God's heart to His people, giving guidance to believers in the body, giving revelation, as well as, often, interpretation, application, and timing. The prophet must take care to be mindful of pride and arrogance. Some prophetic people exalt themselves and the words they speak instead of remaining humble servants of the body.

Evangelist

An evangelist carries a great burden for those who are not a part of the Kingdom of God, as well as an anointing to preach the gospel to them. Their utmost desire is to see people come into the Kingdom. Evangelists are crucial for numeric growth in the local church.

Pastor

The pastor is the heart of the church. He or she is the shepherd who deeply cares for the sheep, ready to lie down everything for them. The pastor wants them to be fed, to grow, to be equipped, to develop their giftings, and to step into the calling of God. Pastors are the bridge between different offices and functions, listening to all sides and restoring calm and order where necessary.

Teacher

Teachers teach and edify the church, imparting divine life and anointing to their listeners who become more hungry for God. Teachers reveal the specifics of the revealed truth. Whereas prophets possess foresight, teachers have impact.

Your influence in the Kingdom of God is guaranteed to be successful when you have cultivated a unified relationship with Him. This puts you in a position of power because the special interests you would be promoting would be of the One God who has all power to effect any change. You represent Him, and, therefore, your governing influence is secure.

Thoughts for Governing Influence:

In the space below, list some additional reflections that you have about your governing influence. How are you being influenced and who are you influencing in the Kingdom?

Chapter 10
The Kingdom-Lordship Principle

Our role is to take back territory that Satan took because God had dominion over it in the first place. Because Christ is Lord and because we have submitted to His will, we go back to get His territory—His Kingdom—for Him, whether the territory is composed of people or things. Our actions should point to Him being our Lord. Anytime we call someone "lord," we recognize their ownership. For instance, a landlord is someone who owns property and allows others to use the property, usually as a result of some financial arrangement.

A king operates with authority and power (dominion) and functions as lord (ruler over a domain—a territory, property, or geographical region). "Lordship is only one aspect of a king's overall identity and status, but it is one of the most important ones."[1]

As Kingdom leaders, we should acknowledge that Jesus owns our hearts and minds. He is Lord. This awareness is necessary if we are to ever take back His Kingdom from the enemy.

When Jesus is Lord in our lives, we are also heirs to His Kingdom. We have rights to His inheritance, in a way that is similar to how earthly families function. Because we are spiritual sons of God, we are heirs to His territory. Subsequently, it is also our responsibility to maintain and protect the territory for the father. We have to stand spiritually for the territory if someone tries to take it. This is what happens in the spirit realm.

Your position according to the Kingdom-Lordship principle is solid. This position is not up for a vote. Kingdom leaders care for God's Kingdom as proper heirs would. You don't have to worry about anyone voting you out because you don't have a certain skill or a certain set of experiences. God's anointing is sufficient. It is your birthright. God gave you the dominion of that particular realm. He spoke that place to you, and you have absolute authority to oversee it. Nobody can really do anything about it. He owns everything and everyone. We just have to get it back. His wealth is measured by souls and territory, and your task is to enrich the Kingdom.

Effective operation in the Kingdom, in the will of God, positions you high above all nations. You serve the King of kings and Lord of lords. Within His Kingdom, you have the ability to exercise dominion and control over the domain that you possess.

The Kingdom-Lordship Principle states that kingship relates to authority and that lordship relates to ownership, and if a king must have a domain within which to rule, then all true kings must have and own territory. This type of authority is different from the type of authority exercised by presidents and prime ministers of governments. Presidents and prime ministers only have the ability to exercise authority within the government in which they have been elected. They do not own all the property within their jurisdiction. On the other hand, a king personally owns the physical domain over which he or she reigns. This distinguishes him or her as king as well as lord.

As the Maker of the heavens and the earth, God has complete authority and the right to give any portion of His domain to whomever He chooses. He chose to give the earth to man—not as owner—but as ruler, manager, and steward. The Lordship of God's Son Jesus was also by His creative rights and was a natural result of Jesus' role in His pre-existence before coming to earth.

> *"In the beginning God created the heavens and the earth." (Genesis 1:1)*

> *"In the beginning was the Word, and the Word was with God, and the Word was God...The Word became flesh and made His dwelling among us. We have seen His glory, the glory of the One and Only, who came from the Father, full of grace and truth."*
> *(John 1:1, 14)*

> *"But in these last days He has spoken to us by His Son, whom He appointed heir of all things, and through whom He made the universe. The Son is the radiance of God's glory and the exact representation of His being, sustaining all things by His powerful Word." (Hebrews 1:2-3a NIV)*

As we operate in the Kingdom-Lordship principle, we operate as His representatives, as suggested in the chapter on governing influence. In His Kingdom government, we govern in a way that makes others want Him to be their owner, to be their Lord. However, the only way to accept Jesus as Lord is through the power of the Holy Spirit:

> *". . .no one can say, "Jesus is Lord," except by the Holy Spirit." (I Corinthians 12:3b)*

From a Kingdom standpoint, the most important thing we can do is confess Jesus as Lord and Savior. Understanding Kingdom-Lordship requires a complete understanding that Jesus is Lord over everything; that includes our lives and our destiny, and it requires our total obedience.

> *"If you confess with your mouth the Lord Jesus and believe in your heart that God has raised Him from the dead, you will be saved." (Romans 10:9)*

This type of confession must be made with deep personal conviction where there is no hesitation, and it must include repentance from sin and total trust in Jesus alone as your Lord and the only hope of salvation. He is the One to whom you must be totally committed.

In practical terms, when thinking about living under the authority of a lord, it would be similar to living in rental property under the authority of a landlord, as alluded to at the beginning of this chapter. The landlord is the land owner, and in order to continue living in that person's rental property, the renter must be willing to abide by the terms of the rental agreement. The renter agrees and acknowledges that the landlord is the owner of the property, that the renter is responsible for the timely payment of rent, and that the renter is accountable for the care of the property. This agreement is typically done by the signing of a written document called a lease, and that document is legally binding. The renter must be obedient to the terms of the lease agreement in order to continue to live on the property. There can be no lordship without obedience.

In terms of the Kingdom, there can be no obedience without love and commitment to the one whom you have pledged your obedience. Genuine faith and love of Christ produces obedience.

> *"If you love Me, keep My commandments."*
> *(John 14:15)*

> *"But why do you call Me 'Lord, Lord,' and do not do the things which I say?" (Luke 6:46)*

When you declare Jesus as your Lord, you are acknowledging His authority over you. You are agreeing that it is your responsibility to be obedient to Him, and that you will be accountable for the care of His Kingdom as His representative.

If He is truly Lord in your life, then He is first in every area. Simply saying He is Lord isn't sufficient for His Lordship. When He is truly Lord, you cannot say such things as, "Lord, but...," or "Lord, except...," or "Lord, wait..." All that can really be said is, "Lord, yes!"

Thoughts for the Kingdom-Lordship Principle:

Consider your relationship with Jesus as King and Lord of your life. In the space below, list some personal reflections about how the Kingdom-Lordship Principle operates and how you can better live a life that is consistent with this principle.

Chapter 11
Stewardship—Not Ownership

"For all that is in heaven and in earth is Yours; Yours is the kingdom, O LORD, and You are exalted as head over all. Both riches and honor come from You, and You reign over all. In Your hand is power and might; in Your hand it is to make great and to give strength to all." (1 Chronicles 29:11b-12)

When you are confident in the Lordship of the Lord, it isn't hard to comprehend what your true position is and how to operate in it.

As God's representative in the earth realm, our position and responsibility is to be that of steward over everything that He has given us charge and trust over. In a general domestic sense, a steward is personally responsible for taking care of another person's property or financial affairs. It is the conducting, supervising, or managing of something, especially the careful and responsible management of something entrusted to one's care.[1]

"The earth is the LORD's, and all its fullness, the world and those who dwell therein. For He has founded it upon the waters. Who may ascend into the hill of the LORD? Or who may stand in His holy place? He who has not lifted up his soul to an idol, nor sworn deceitfully." (Psalm 24:1-4)

God has entrusted those who are His representatives, His ambassadors, His co-workers, and His servants with the charge of being concerned with how to best manage His possessions.

A servant, in the domestic sense of the word, has typically been used to describe the responsibility of a household employee. This term is also expanded to include a household employee's responsibility for managing domestic affairs and for the responsibility of taking general care of something owned by someone else.

Ownership, on the other hand, emphasizes possession, title, rights, and proprietorship. The earth and everything in it belongs to the Lord Jehovah. He created it. He is the proprietor and has all rights to it. As such, He has legal title over it. God created man in His image and likeness. We are His creation. Therefore, we also belong to Him.

People often use terms such as, "I own this." "It's mine because I earned the money and I paid for it." The question that really needs to be examined is whether we really own anything at all.

For the servants of the household of God, we have to recognize that He owns everything and that all blessings come from Him. When we are able to see things from this perspective, then we are able to view ourselves more in the role of stewards. On the other hand, if we continuously view ourselves as owners of what we think we have earned and paid for, then we will think of every other thing in our lives the same way. It's only natural to think of yourself as being the one in charge, especially when it's your home, it's your money, it's your talent, it's your life, and you own it all.

As stewards, we need only to concern ourselves with how to best manage God's possessions. When we can change our thinking to truly be that of a steward, then the management of money, cars, houses and talents are no longer our possessions. They all belong to the Lord; we just manage it all for Him.

Jesus was the only One capable of successfully being able to pay the price for God's possessions. After all, He owns everything, and it was His shed blood that redeemed us and paid the penalty for our salvation from sin. It is for this reason that we have been graced with the privilege of being God's representatives—His servants and stewards—in the earth realm.

"For we are God's fellow workers; you are God's field, you are God's building. According to the grace of God which was given to me, as a wise master builder I have laid the foundation, and another builds on it. But let each one take heed how he builds on it. For no other foundation can anyone lay than that which is laid, which is Jesus Christ." (1 Corinthians 3:9-11)

Many have built for themselves homes, businesses, empires, ministries, and wealth with what they believed was by their own hands, intelligence, and means. However, Jesus is the Master Builder and the Chief Cornerstone. He was the One who purchased it all for us and then designed the foundation for us. We are simply charged with building upon that foundation through the preached Word of God, and having done so, then to teach, baptize, and make disciples of all nations. This is how we are to build God's Kingdom.

> *"Therefore it is also contained in the Scripture, 'Behold, I lay in Zion a chief cornerstone, elect, precious, and he who believes on Him will by no means be put to shame.' Therefore, to you who believe, He is precious; but to those who are disobedient, 'The stone which the builders rejected has become the chief cornerstone,' and 'a stone of stumbling and a rock of offense.' They stumble, being disobedient to the word, to which they also were also appointed." (1 Peter 2:6-8)*

What is imperative to know is that anyone choosing not to believe in Him, to those individuals He is a "stone of stumbling and a rock of offense." Jesus is either the means of salvation for those who believe in Him, or He is the means of judgment for those who choose to reject Him.

If there is a question to be asked at this point, that question should be, "What are we to be stewards of?" The answer is very easy: everything that God has entrusted and delegated to us. That includes everything from this present day, from your talents and abilities to your authority, from your family to your homes, from your friendships to your responsibilities.[2]

Everything is given to us from and by God, either directly or through the use of the gifts, tools, and intelligence that He has given us. Inasmuch as He is the Ruler and Controller over everything in a believer's life, then He can, therefore, be trusted to change any type of unhealthy behavior or habit that we may have. That includes all of our spending and eating habits, all fears and anxieties, all decision making and all relationship issues—familial and otherwise.

Your position of steward now allows you to acknowledge that you can release and transfer ownership of that which you believed was yours to its rightful owner, the Lord God. He is a spiritual God, and, therefore, all decisions made at this point must now be spiritual ones. He is the Lord God and is Spiritual Ruler of it all and must be conferred and consulted with, through continual prayer, for all decisions that must be made.

"Trust in the LORD with all your heart, and lean not on your own understanding; in all your ways acknowledge Him, and He shall direct your paths. Do not be wise in your own eyes." (Proverbs 3:5-7a)

The Lord directs all our ways and paths (notice that the terms *ways* and *paths* in this Scripture are both plural). He leads us in every direction and in every decision when He has all of our things transferred to Him.

Some may be of the opinion that because they are already serving God in various ways that God automatically honors and blesses their decisions. For example, if they are already serving in positions of leadership and authority, already scholars and teachers of the Word, and already have what they believe to be an exemplary prayer life, they might think that they have met the requirements to be blessed by God in whatever they choose to do, even if He was not consulted prior to the decision being made.

We must realize that there is absolutely no substitute for returning our possessions to God, even our decision-making. If we believe that we are the owners of even a single possession or decision, then the events affecting that possession or decision are going to affect our attitudes. God will not force His will upon us. He will not input His perfect will into our lives unless we first surrender our wills to Him. However, if we make a total transfer of everything to God, then He will demonstrate His ability.[3]

"Let a man so consider us, as servants of Christ and stewards of the mysteries of God. Moreover it is required in stewards that one be found faithful."
(1 Corinthians 4:1-2)

"Therefore you shall be careful to do as the LORD your God has commanded you; you shall not turn aside to the right hand or to the left. You shall walk in all the ways which the LORD your God has commanded you, that you may live and that it may be well with you, and that you may prolong your days in the land which you shall possess." (Deuteronomy 5:32-33)

It may seem very easy to say that you will make a total transfer of everything to God; it may not be so easy to actually do it. The American culture is bred in instilling the "American Dream" into the minds of its citizens. It is possible that the dream of home and business ownership and the drive for the accumulation of wealth and financial prosperity may be responsible for causing untold numbers of people to go into debt, taking on unhealthy spending habits and stress, anxiety, and fear. As the late Dr. Myles Munroe said,

"The dream began as a notion that every person has the right to pursue happiness, and the freedom to strive for a better life through hard work and fair ambition. But over time, this dream has come to represent a set of expectations about owning things and making money."[4]

The expansive belief in the possibilities of the American dream is deeply embedded in the country's psyche, and it is a compelling message that our political leaders call on whenever the country is in crisis. We are reminded of our 'can-do' spirit, and that individuals have the power to bring about change.[5] However, true freedom and the realization of a transformation only comes when God is allowed to guide you.

Making the transfer from the ownership dream to the stewardship reality is as simple as making a resolute and unwavering decree and declaration.

Decree and declare the following:

I decree and declare to the Lord God, this day (fill in the date), that:

- I will hereby transfer to the Lord the ownership of the following possessions: (make a list of everything that you will be transferring);
- I now am a steward of the possessions listed above and relinquish all rights, interest, and ownership of the above and understand that this release and surrender is irrevocable;
- Jesus is the true Ruler and Controller over everything in my life. He owns everything and all blessings come from Him;

- Inasmuch as Jesus is the Owner, He can be trusted to change every type of unhealthy behavior and habit that I may have including all of my spending and eating habits, all of my fears and anxieties, all of my decision making and all of my relationship issues—emotional, familial, personal, business, casual, and otherwise.

Consider making it a formal declaration by putting it in writing. You may even desire to make yourself accountable by adding witnesses to sign and attest to your decree and declaration.

You are now ready to assume your Kingdom position.

Thoughts for Stewardship—Not Ownership:

Look at the list that you made of the things that you thought you owned that you will now transfer to God. Take some time to think about what your life will be like now that you are a steward and not an owner. In the space below, write your reflections about this new way of living.

Chapter 12
Assuming Your Position of Kingdom Leadership

"He who dwells in the secret place of the Most High shall abide under the shadow of the Almighty. I will say of the LORD, 'He is my refuge and my fortress; My God, in Him I will trust.'" (Psalm 91:1-2)

"For thus says the High and Lofty One Who inhabits eternity, whose name is Holy; I dwell in the high and holy place, with him who has a contrite and humble spirit, to revive the spirit of the humble, and to revive the heart of the contrite ones.'" (Isaiah 57:15)

The Kingdom position is in the place of humility and worship, bowing before the Lord your Maker. In order to assume your Kingdom position, it is important to be aware of God's position requirements. Knowing your Kingdom position requires acknowledgement of who the King truly is in your life. The God that we serve is the Most High God, and the secret place of His habitation is a place of divine protection, peace, and power where He sits high and is lifted up. In this place, He cannot be reached by anyone—unless He specifically decrees it.

This secret place is His ascended place of rest, and the one who is positioned next to Him in this high and lifted place is high and lifted up along with Him. In the presence of God, the enemy has no access, and by dwelling in this place and being positioned with Him, you are assured of His shielded protection. God will shield you with His presence and make evil powerless before you.[1]

Everything and everyone is subject to the Lord, even the ones who choose not to acknowledge Him. But even they will eventually confess Him as Lord, just as Paul said when he quoted Isaiah 45:23. The Father and the Son, along with the Holy Spirit, are so high that even their enemies shall one day acknowledge it.

"Therefore God has also highly exalted Him and given Him the name which is above every name, that at the name of Jesus every knee should bow, of those in heaven, and of those on earth, and of those under the earth, and that every tongue should confess that Jesus Christ is Lord, to the glory of God the Father." (Philippians 2:9-11)

When you abide and are positioned with God you are automatically concealed by the cloud of His glory. This is where the shadow of Shaddai will overshadow you. Shaddai is a Hebrew descriptor for God, meaning *sustainer*, *provider*, or some other attributes of God. Just as we can be surrounded by the 'shadow of death' (see Psalm 23), so we can be surrounded by the 'shadow of Shaddai.' Like a powerful eagle brooding over her chicks, so Shaddai covers you with wings of protection.[1]

Therefore, at any given moment of our day, regardless of our circumstances, we can attune ourselves to the reality of the Divine Presence and come boldly before the throne of grace. The world knows nothing of this realm and is enslaved by appearances.[2]

In serving the Lord in whatever capacity you serve in ministry, you may have asked yourself one or more of these questions: "Am I serving in a place that is most effective?" "Am I fulfilling my purpose?" "What should I really be doing, and how should I be doing it?" "Is God really pleased with my service?" Moreover, if you have been struggling in some particular area or areas of your life, you may have asked yourself one or more of these questions: "Why does it seem as though I am always under attack?" "When will my breakthrough finally come?" "How long will this season of struggling continue?"

Your Kingdom position places you in an area where these types of questions are put into their proper perspective. In the article on ownership versus stewardship, the author writes that whoever, or whatever, is "highest in your heart will be highest in your worship."[3] "Whatever you give the most attention to is where you will make your consistent sacrifices. Whatever is highest in your heart will receive honor and glory from your life. Whatever you exalt receives the authority to edify (build up, strengthen) your life. When we exalt God, He shows us how to navigate through our problems and pitfalls. When we exalt our situations and issues, we stay entangled in the 'stuff' we were called to live above."[4]

The position you are to assume in the Kingdom is in terms of

1. Putting God first in everything and in every situation, and
2. Committing yourself to prayer and worshiping Him only.

The disciples asked many questions of Jesus, but the question most prevalent on their minds was whom Jesus, the One they had been following, would name as being the greatest in the Kingdom. Their focus was not on the Kingdom; they were more concerned with appearances.

> *"At that time the disciples came to Jesus, saying, 'Who then is greatest in the kingdom of heaven?' Then Jesus called a little child to Him, set him in the midst of them, and said, 'Assuredly, I say to you, unless you are converted and become as little children, you will by no means enter the kingdom of heaven. Therefore whoever humbles himself as this little child is the greatest in the kingdom of heaven. Whoever receives one little child like this in My name receives Me.'"*
> *(Matthew 18:1-5)*

The disciples were trying to find out who was the greatest in the Kingdom, but like many, they did not understand the true nature of God's Kingdom. They were expecting that Jesus's mission was to depose the Roman government, bring freedom to the Jews, and then establish a new earthly realm.

Jesus's explanation for who was the greatest was probably not what they wanted to hear. It was not likely that a child would ever be able to hold a high position in anything. Children were most likely to be responsible only for helping their families by being obedient, not by being in charge of running things and certainly not by holding positions of power. As a child, I remember being told the adage that children were to be seen and not heard.

What should have been obvious to the disciples is that the greatest individual in any kingdom is, of course, the King.[5] Jesus came as a humble servant. He was the example that they were to emulate.

One of the enemy's tactics is to accuse you and attack an exaggerated sense of your own self-righteousness. If you fall for these tactics, then it is likely that you may not be able to view yourself from an honest perspective. We know Who lives in us, but we must also know what is in us in order to be successful in our Kingdom walk.

The Kingdom position that Jesus was describing to His disciples was two-fold. That position requires that followers of Christ should be

1. Converted as little children

"As newborn babes, desire the pure milk of the word, that you may grow." (1 Peter 2:2)

and

2. Humble

"But he who is greatest among you shall be your servant. And whoever exalts himself will be humbled, and he who humbles himself will be exalted." (Matthew 23:11-12)

Conversion requires that a person be changed from just being a Christian or not being one at all to becoming an active believer and turning from their current ways. That turning must be away from those things that are inconsistent with a relationship with God and turning to God by giving Him His rightful place in his or her life.[6] Your conversion has to be a total changeover.

What is important in Matthew 23: 11–12 is that Jesus was not speaking about a place of position or power in the Kingdom. He was clearly saying that your Kingdom position is one of humility and joyous service—and this was the position required to even enter into the Kingdom.

The desire of the 'newborn babe' in 1 Peter 2:2 speaks to your desire for the nourishment of the pure Word of God. Newborns require proper nourishment in order to grow and develop. The Word is our source of growth and development, and its purity should not be watered down or fabricated by carnal [worldly and earthly desires and appetites of the flesh or body][7] thoughts or ideas.

For a newborn, the mother's milk is naturally the purest milk, and it provides the best nutrients for the child. It also provides the child with all the natural antibodies needed to protect it from germs and illnesses. This milk is untouched and can only become corrupted by what the mother consumes.

Our modern world has created laboratory formulas as a substitute for the mother's natural milk. The formula serves as a quick and convenient replacement for mothers who cannot, or choose to not, nurse their children. This laboratory substitute lacks the mother's natural ability to provide the necessary antibodies to protect and ward off infections and germs.

Our God is pure and undefiled, He operates in all truth, and His Word is truth. His truth is revealed to us through the Scriptures. Although God requires that we should seek Him first, some may have chosen to seek the 'formula' [fabricated in carnality] of the Word instead of through Him directly.

The deep things of God are revealed through His Holy Spirit. After reading and studying the Word, the Spirit will provide understanding and will bring all things to your remembrance, but you have to put forth the effort to read and study the Word consistently. The Spirit cannot help you to re-member that which you have never made a member of your body through reading, studying, and meditating.

Taking Your Position

"I have raised my hand to the LORD, God Most High, the Possessor of heaven and earth."
(Genesis 14:22b)

The list below brings together the major points in this chapter that highlight how to assume your Kingdom position:

1. Put God and His Kingdom first, in and above everything; worshiping Him and Him only;
2. Be converted, as little children;
3. Consistently read, study and meditate on the Word of God to maintain growth, nourishment and strength;
4. Remain humble and prayerful; and
5. Be obedient to His leading; even if it seems illogical to the world.

Thoughts for Assuming Your Kingdom Position:

On the following page, list some additional reflections you have about your Kingdom position and the necessity for humility and worship. Indicate the plan and the steps you will take in assuming your rightful Kingdom position.

Conclusion

In order to be the kind of leader that God requires, you have to be more than someone with an MBA. In fact, college degrees do not figure into God's requirements for leadership. In this book, I have shared with you that God requires a special kind of leader, a Kingdom leader.

Kingdom leaders are people who gain an understanding of who they are in God. We began the book with the Kingdom Genomes chapter in which I pointed out that we were made to be kings because we were made in God's image. It is in our spiritual DNA to be leaders.

Then, the concept of Kingdom Citizenship was unpacked, along with Kingdom Kingship. You below in God's Kingdom. In fact, you were designed to be a king. Don't give up your rights to both experiences just because others do not understand your place in the Kingdom. Embrace who you are and the power that is at your disposal.

The first three concepts are foundational to all the rest. With the concepts of Kingdom genomes, citizenship, and kingship as the base of our understanding, all the others can develop. One who is moving from the average leadership model to a Kingdom leadership model transforms his or her mindset, attitude, and character. The goal of such a change should not be money or other earthly benefits. You just might have those. There is nothing to say that you can't. However, financial benefits in themselves are not the goal of adopting a life of Kingdom leadership. The purpose for taking on this lifestyle is so that you will be consistent with what God designed you to be.

Kingdom leaders who desire to operate in God's perfect will and with complete authority and power must be mindful of God's requirements. He desires total obedience to His commands—this demonstrates our sincere love and devotion to Him. He desires that you give. In fact, He desires you to leave behind the idea that you own anything. You are simply a steward of what God has allowed you to have responsibility for. Only responsible stewards are fit to lead as God would have them do. Only when you are free of your neighbor's empty search for things and their protection can you garner the level of trust that you need to effectively lead in your territory of influence.

You can assume your position of Kingdom leadership. In this book, you have the tools to help you to navigate the road to becoming the kind of leader that God needs you to be. The principles outlined in this book represent the blueprint for effective Kingdom administration. I leave you with a synopsis of each principle. I pray that you find them transformative in a way that will lead you to embrace your role and power as a Kingdom leader.

1. Kingdom genomes identify how you are different from others while still having full authority to act on God's behalf because we share in His nature and have His communicable attributes.
2. Kingdom citizenship and kingship are our rights, according to the Word of God. Success in the Kingdom is guaranteed by knowledge and authority of the Word of God as well as the extension of power from God to be victorious over all the powers of the enemy.
3. A Kingdom mindset requires that you think like a king and understand the characteristics of a king.

4. Kingdom attitude reflects the image of Christ's righteousness and the need for seeking God's righteousness.
5. Kingdom character requires an understanding of Kingdom thoughts and perceptions.
6. Transformation leads to the reinstatement of the power that God always meant for His people to have. He always intended us to have dominion and authority.
7. A Kingdom atmosphere identifies your position next to Christ in heavenly places.
8. The keys of the Kingdom provide unlimited access God's power. With the gifts (the keys) that God has given us, we must go forth to preach the gospel with power to unlock the spiritual truths of the Word.
9. Your governing influence is dependent upon unity with God through complete obedience and positioning yourself under His anointing in order to be the recipient of His blessings.
10. The Kingdom-Lordship principle solidifies your identity and rightful authority to exercise dominion over the earth.
11. You were designed to be a steward, not an owner. Embracing the Stewardship—Not Ownership principle solidifies your servant position by acknowledging who the true Owner is and the need for conferring and consulting with Him on all decisions through continual prayer.
12. Assuming your Kingdom position puts you in the place of habitation along with Christ in heavenly places. It is in this place where you are automatically concealed by the cloud of God's glory and are assured of safety from the enemy.

Thank you for reading this book. I trust that you enjoyed experiencing God in renewed ways. He desires so much to fellowship with us because He loves us.

End Notes

Chapter One
1. "What Does God Look Like?" www.allaboutgod.com/what-does-god-look-like (Accessed 2/28/2015)
2. Rice University. "Genomic Frontier–The Unexplored Animal Kingdom." December 19, 2013. www.sciencedaily.com/releases
3. "What is a Genome?" Your introduction to DNA, Genes and Genomes. www.yourgenome.org/dgg/general/genomes

Chapter Two
1. The American Heritage Dictionary of the English Language. Kingship; page 722. American Heritage Publishing Company, Inc. 1970.
2. Dr. Myles Monroe. "Kingdom Principles–Preparing for Kingdom Experience and Expansion." Chapter Six, Page 119. 2006.
3. Ibid. Page 120.

Chapter Three
1. Kingdom. Google definition. (Accessed 12/8/2014)

Chapter Four
1. www.jesuschristsavior.net. "The Eight Beatitudes of Jesus."
2. www.psychologytoday.com. "The Key Difference Between Pride and Arrogance" by Guy Winch, Ph.D. July 29, 2014.

Chapter Five
1. Dr. Amanda Goodson. "Kingdom Character." Page 12, 15. 2012.

2. Ibid. Page 12.
3. Ibid. Page 18.
4. Ibid. Page 50.
5. Ibid. Page 54.
6. Ibid. Page 62.
7. Ibid. Page 65.
8. Ibid. Page 68.
9. Ibid. Page 72.
10. Ibid. Page 59.

Chapter Six
1. www.Scriptureinsights.com. "Be Transformed by the Renewing of Your Minds." James L. Morrisson. (Accessed 1/7/2015)
2. Francis Frangipane. "The Three Battlegrounds." Page 41. Arrow Publications. 2000.
3. www.Scriptureinsights.com. "Be Transformed by the Renewing of Your Minds." James L. Morrisson. (Accessed 1/7/2015)

Chapter Seven
1. "An Atmosphere Conducive for God's Presence to Come" Biblical Study Outline. PDF. (Accessed 1/7/2015)
2. Uzziah Tablet Inscription. http://www.bible-history.com/archaeology/israel/uzziah-tablet.html (Accessed 1/12/2015)

Chapter Eight
1. Dr. Myles Monroe. "Kingdom Principles–Preparing for Kingdom Experience and Expansion." Chapter Nine, Page 157. 2006.

Chapter Eleven
1. Ownership vs. Stewardship. Achieve Complete Financial Freedom. www.howtogainwealth.com. (Accessed 2/17/2015)

2. Ibid.
3. Ibid.
4. Kate Ellis and Ellen Guettler. "A Better Life–Creating the American Dream." American Dream–American Radioworks. www.americanradioworks.publicradio.org (Accessed 2/21/2015)
5. Ibid. Introduction.

Chapter Twelve
1. John J. Parsons. "Secret of the Most High–Dwelling in the Shadow of Shaddai." www.hebrew4christians.com/Meditations/Secret/secret.html (Accessed 2/23/2015)
2. Ibid.
3. Ownership vs. Stewardship. Achieve Complete Financial Freedom. www.howtogainwealth.com. (Accessed 2/17/2015)
4. LaBryant Friend, Senior Pastor. "Jehovah El Elyon–The God Most High." Mount Calvary Baptist Church. February 22, 2015.
5. Ryan J. Hale. "Position in the Kingdom". http://kingdom.ryanjhale.com/2013/07/20/position-in-the-kingdom/ (Accessed 2/21/2015)
6. "What Does it Mean to be Converted and Born Again?" www.christianity.co.nz/born1.htm (Accessed 2/21/2015)
7. The American Heritage Dictionary of the English Language. Carnal; page 205. American Heritage Publishing Company, Inc. 1970.

About the Author

Dr. Amanda Goodson

Dr. Amanda H. Goodson is a native of Decatur, Alabama and currently resides in Tucson, Arizona where she is a leader in her church.

Goodson is a certified coach, speaker, trainer and the Bountiful Life television show host. She is a published author of several books.

Dr. Goodson is fully committed to the Lord and knows that she has a blessed Spirit-led life. Her purpose is to fill the earth with the knowledge of God's glory by serving the Lord boldly through her ministry, bringing others closer to Christ and introducing Him to those who have not accepted Him as their personal Savior. God's Word is her authority.

Dr. Goodson has a Bachelor of Science degree in Electrical Engineering, a Master of Science degree in Management, and a Doctor of Ministry.

She and her family enjoy their ministry work for the Kingdom.

For further information or to book Dr. Goodson, please contact her at:

AmandaGoodson.com

Books by Dr. Amanda Goodson

Spiritual Quickbooks ™
Kingdom Character
Spiritual Authority
Carmel Voices
The Power to Make an Impact
Powerful People Follow Christ
Step out in Faith
Going Higher, Declarations for Kids
On the Rise
Spiritual Intelligence
Switch to Holiness

Spiritual Workbooks
Switch to Holiness Workbook

Leadership Minibooks ™
The Authority of a Leader
Character of a Leader
Unlock Your Full Potential
12 Power Principles for Administrative Professionals
Soar to Your Destiny

Leadership Workbooks
Unlock Your Full Potential Workbook

www.ingramcontent.com/pod-product-compliance
Lightning Source LLC
LaVergne TN
LVHW041631070426
835507LV00008B/552